DISCOVERY WALKS
in
LANCASHIRE

Brian Conduit

Published by Sigma Leisure – an imprint of
Sigma Press, 1 South Oak Lane, Wilmslow, Cheshire SK9 6AR, England.

British Library Cataloguing in Publication Data
A CIP record for this book is available from the British Library.

ISBN: 1-85058-658-6

Typesetting and Design by: Sigma Press, Wilmslow, Cheshire.

Cover Design: The Agency, Macclesfield
Cover photographs: larger picture – the Wycoller Valley; top left – Sawley Abbey; bottom left – Stonyhurst. *All Photographs: Brian Conduit*

Maps: Jeremy Semmens

Printed by: MFP Design and Print

Disclaimer: the information in this book is given in good faith and is believed to be correct at the time of publication. No responsibility is accepted by either the author or publisher for errors or omissions, or for any loss or injury howsoever caused. Only you can judge your own fitness, competence and experience.

Preface

Before I came to live in the Ribble Valley over 30 years ago, my first-hand knowledge of Lancashire consisted of a couple of teenage holidays in Blackpool, a rail excursion to Southport on a grey August Bank Holiday Monday, and a one-day visit to a relative temporarily living in a Manchester suburb. None of these experiences came anywhere near to preparing me for the Lancashire that I have subsequently discovered – a county of outstanding and varied scenic beauty coupled with a wide range of historic attractions.

Having travelled and walked extensively in most parts of Britain, I have reached the conclusion that some of the finest countryside is to be found on my own doorstep, a conclusion further reinforced while preparing this book. Short walks from my home can take me onto the slopes of witch-haunted Pendle Hill or along the banks of the delightful River Ribble. After a few minutes in the car, I can be driving through the rugged grandeur of the Forest of Bowland. Slightly longer journeys bring me to the open expanses of the western Pennines, the gentler terrain of the Lune valley and the tree-fringed coast of Morecambe Bay.Where else in the country could I find such scenic variety within comparatively short distances?

The areas just mentioned are the obvious gems for walkers but in the following selection of walks, I have not neglected the flat country of the coastal plain or those parts of south Lancashire now lost to Greater Manchester and Merseyside, all of which have their unique appeal. Even within the most urbanised areas, it is perhaps surprising how many attractive rural oases can still be found.

Scattered throughout these differing landscapes are the many relics of the past and the walks have been chosen to embrace as many of these as possible. They include Roman remains, ruined medieval abbeys and castles, Tudor manor houses and inevitably the monuments that illustrate the major role played by Lancashire in the Industrial Revolution.

Although this is predominantly a book of country walks, I have featured short walks in the two major cities, Manchester and Liverpool, and in Lancaster, the county's major historic town. Urban walks can be both satisfying and rewarding, add interest and variety and are certainly worth considering on a wet day.

Whether strolling by the banks of the Ribble or Lune, admiring the Georgian architecture of Lancaster, or striding across the West Pennine Moors, I hope that you will enjoy exploring on foot – the only way you can really get to know an area – one of England's most absorbing counties.

Brian Conduit

Contents

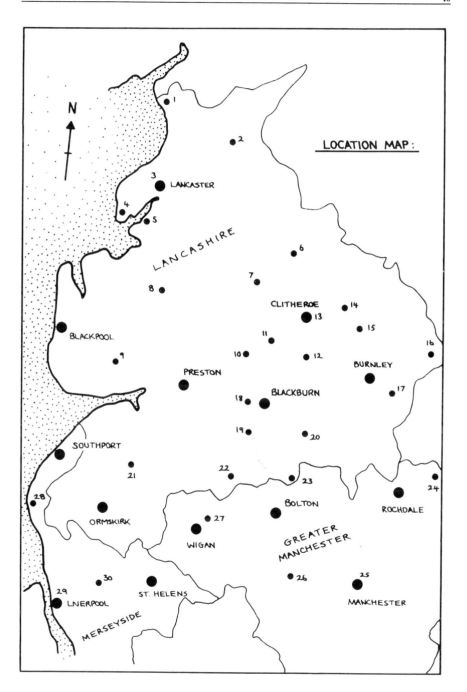

Introduction

This walking guide covers not just the present administrative county of Lancashire but also those parts of Greater Manchester and Merseyside that were in Lancashire prior to the boundary changes of 1974. Throughout this area there is much to discover and all the walks have some sort of heritage theme. Apart from the three urban walks – in Lancaster, Manchester and Liverpool – they also pass through landscapes that range from pleasant to magnificent. Fine scenery coupled with historic appeal are the ideal ingredients for satisfying and memorable walks and it is hoped that the following selection all fall within that category.

Images of Lancashire

Despite this varied abundance of heritage and scenery, Lancashire tends to be somewhat undervalued as a walking area, at least by many people from outside the county who often hurry through it at weekends on their way to more crowded and congested destinations in the Lake District, Yorkshire Dales and Peak District. Perhaps it suffers from having three outstanding national parks literally on the doorstep – although it does possess two areas of outstanding natural beauty as well as plenty of country parks – but it probably suffers more from a false and outdated image.

When non-Lancastrians think of Lancashire, the images that are most likely to spring to mind are cobbled streets, 'dark Satanic mills', tightly-packed industrial towns, Blackpool Tower and Test Matches rained off at Old Trafford. The images that are more familiar to local walkers and which feature strongly in this guide are the beauties of the Ribble and Lune valleys, Forest of Bowland, Morecambe Bay coast and the West Pennine Moors; the Georgian elegance of Lancaster, and a collection of attractive villages that can stand comparison with those of the nearby Yorkshire Dales or even the Cotswolds.·

I have to confess that I had the same false images when I first came to live and work in the county over 30 years ago but a few initial excursions out to the Ribble valley and through the Trough of Bowland soon opened my eyes and taught me the error of my ways. For walkers the most impressive feature of the Lancashire landscape is the superb and tremendously varied terrain, within which are a wealth of historic sites and monuments from the Roman period to the Industrial Revolution. An added bonus is that, compared with some other parts of Britain, this outstanding countryside is easily accessible from the nearby urban areas.

There can be few counties in England that can boast Lancashire's variety of scenery. Starting in the north west corner, the Arnside and Silverdale Area of Outstanding Natural Beauty, an area of wooded limestone hills fringing the shoreline of Morecambe Bay, straddles the border with Cumbria and provides superb views of the south Lakeland fells. The coast can be followed around to the flat and fertile country of the Fylde, situated between the Lune and Ribble estuaries, and southwards across the Ribble to the reclaimed marshes and mosses of the West Lancashire plain. Here is to be found an almost Fenland landscape which continues down to Liverpool and the Mersey estuary and borders a coastline renowned for its expanses of dunes and pine woods to the south of Southport.

From their estuaries, the Lune and Ribble flow through verdant and unspoilt valleys, occupied by the county's prettiest villages, towards the line of the Pennines. Between them is one of the westerly bulges of the Pennines, the Forest of Bowland, a wild, lonely and almost empty region, with hills that rise to over 1800ft. Here is to be found some of the most challenging walks in Lancashire and together with witch-haunted Pendle Hill – physically detached from it by the Ribble valley – the Forest of Bowland makes up the county's second area of outstanding natural beauty.

As the Pennines continue southwards, another bulge – the West Pennine Moors – thrusts westwards towards the coastal plain. These austere, sometimes bleak and windswept uplands are encircled by Blackburn, Accrington, the Irwell valley, Bury, Bolton and Chorley and include the old hunting ground of the Forest of Rossendale. It was in the valleys below these moors that the cotton industry developed and large industrial towns grew up, for whose inhabitants the moors were the easiest – and indeed the only – access to open country. Their bareness is broken up by attractive wooded valleys or cloughs and the landscape is enhanced by a series of reservoirs which create an almost mini-Lake District.

The line of the Pennines proceeds southwards into the more heavily built up Greater Manchester but there are still pockets of open country here, some of which have been reclaimed from industry, and from the moorland heights, the extensive views across the urban sprawl of Manchester and its satellite towns extend to the distant rim of the Peak District.

History

Throughout this varied terrain stand the many monuments to Lancashire's history. A few vestiges of the Roman origins of Manchester and Lancaster survive and there is a stretch of reputed Roman road on the Pennine moors above Rochdale, but the county's principal Roman remains are the fort and bath house at Ribchester. There are medieval castles at Lancaster, Clitheroe and Greenhalgh and a later castle at Hornby. Lancashire possesses no great medieval cathedral but monastic ruins can be seen at Cockersand, Sawley and Whalley.

Until the Industrial Revolution, Lancashire was a relatively poor and sparsely populated county and therefore lacks any large and imposing stately homes on the scale of, say, Chatsworth or Blenheim. As compensation, there are a large number of splendid manor houses and modest country mansions, dating from the late medieval to the Victorian period, scattered throughout the valleys, moorlands and coastal lowlands. Lancaster can claim to contain some of the finest Georgian architecture in the country, a legacy of its former prosperity as a port, and further reminders of its 18th-century heyday can be seen at Sunderland Point and Glasson Dock lower down the Lune estuary. More than anything else it was the Industrial Revolution, and in particular the tremendous growth of the cotton industry, that transformed the county. All school history books explain the main advantages that Lancashire possessed to become the principal centre of cotton manufacturing in Britain: abundant water power, coal resources, damp climate and proximity to west coast ports, chiefly Liverpool. Evidence of the impact of the Industrial Revolution can be seen all over the region but principally in the superb collection of 19th-century civic monuments in Liverpool and Manchester, and the many mill buildings – large and small – found mostly within a 30 mile radius of Manchester, the commercial centre of the cotton industry.

Industrial expansion required transport improvements and Lancashire can claim to be one of the major birthplaces of both the canals and railways. Several of the walks make use of stretches of canal towpath and at the Castlefield Urban Heritage Park in the centre of Manchester, the termini of the world's first canal and railway are within a few metres of each other and in close proximity to the remains of a Roman fort.

Much of Lancashire's traditional industry has gone and has become part of history. Some of the walks illustrate this change and take you through a largely post-industrial landscape where redundant industrial and commercial sites, such as the Albert Dock in Liverpool and Wigan Pier, have been put to other uses and areas of industrial dereliction have been reclaimed and been made green and pleasant again.

Enjoy these walks that not only give you superb scenery but also help you to explore and appreciate more fully the rich historic legacy of one of England's most varied counties. As stated at the beginning of this introduction, there is much to discover.

General Information

All the walks follow either public rights of way or other routes to which walkers traditionally have access: waymarked permissive paths, canal towpaths, country parks and access areas. Road walking has been kept to a minimum. Many walks use stretches of some of the long distance and recreational paths in the county – Ribble Way, Lancashire Coastal Way, Pendle Way, Rossendale Way – that have the advantage of usually being well waymarked. The routes can be walked at any time of the year but it is best to avoid the exposed moorland walks in bad weather, especially misty conditions. Mud is likely to be the main hazard, especially in winter or after a prolonged rainy spell, and you should always be prepared for this and have the appropriate footwear.

As the walks include many sites of historic interest and you will no doubt wish to visit some of these, it is disappointing if you find them closed. Therefore, it is important to check opening times – which vary considerably. Country houses are often closed during the winter months and even during the summer, may have very restricted opening times. The nearest Tourist Information Centre will provide you with the details, as well as up to date information on public transport and hotels, guest houses and bed and breakfast establishments.

Local Tourist Information Centres

Accrington	01254 386807
Blackburn	01254 53277
Blackpool	01253 4782222/403223
Bolton	01204 364333
Burnley	01282 455485
Bury	0161 2535111
Charnock Richard (M6)	01257 793773
Clitheroe	01200 425566
Fleetwood	01253 773953
Forton (M6)	01524 792181
Garstang	01995 602125
Lancaster	01524 32878
Liverpool	0151 7093631/7088854
Lytham St Annes	01253 725610
Manchester	0161 2343157/2343158
Morecambe	01524 582808/582809
Oldham	0161 6271024
Preston	01772 253731
Rawtenstall	01706 226590
Rochdale	01706 356592
Saddleworth	01457 870336
Southport	01704 533333
Wigan	01942 825677

Useful Addresses

North West Tourist Board, Swan House, Swan Meadow Road, Wigan Pier, Wigan WN3 5BB. Tel:01942 821222

National Trust (North West Regional Office), The Hollens, Grasmere, Ambleside, Cumbria LA22 9QZ. Tel:01539 435353

English Heritage, Customer Services, PO Box 9019, London WIA 0JA. Tel:0171 9733434

English Nature, North West Team, Pier House, Wallgate, Wigan WN3 4AL. Tel:01942 820342

Countryside Commission, North West Regional Office, Bridgewater House, Whitworth Street, Manchester M1 6LT. Tel:0161 2371061

Ramblers' Association, 1/5 Wandsworth Road, London SW8 2XX. Tel:0171 5826878

The Country Code

Please observe this when walking in the countryside.

* Enjoy the countryside and respect its life and work

* Guard against all risk of fire

* Take your litter home

* Fasten all gates

* Help to keep all water clean

* Keep your dogs under control

* Protect wildlife, plants and trees

* Keep to public paths across farmland

* Take special care on country roads

* Leave livestock, crops and machinery alone

* Make no unnecessary noise

* Use gates and stiles to cross fences, hedges and walls

1. Silverdale and Leighton Hall

Start/Parking: Silverdale, The Shore car park—grid reference 457749.

Distance: 7½ miles (12.1 km).

Category: Moderate.

Refreshments: Pubs and the Hedgerows Coffee Shop at Silverdale, tea room at RSPB Leighton Moss Visitor Centre, tea room at Waterslack Garden Centre near entrance to Eaves Wood, tea room at Leighton Hall.

Terrain: Easy and generally flat walking mainly on clear field and woodland paths; the final stretch is along the shore of Morecambe Bay

OS Maps: Landranger 97, Pathfinder 636.

Public transport: Buses from Carnforth, Morecambe and Lancaster; Silverdale station is served by trains from Preston, Lancaster and Barrow-in-Furness.

What you'll discover

This is a highly attractive and absorbing walk in the rolling and well-wooded limestone country that adjoins the shores of Morecambe Bay. It takes you across bright green fields criss-crossed by dry-stone walls, through several areas of delightful woodland, and ends with a walk along the shore. The route passes through a variety of nature reserves and there is the opportunity to visit an 18th-century hall. In addition, there are extensive views across Morecambe Bay and at times the profile of the Lakeland mountains can be seen on the horizon.

Route Directions

Start by facing the sea and turn left along Shore Road which curves left to a T-junction. Turn left and take the first turning on the left, sign-posted to Arnside, into Silverdale village **(A)**. Before reaching the church, turn right, at a public footpath sign to Bottoms Lane and The Row, along an enclosed tarmac path, keep ahead along St John's Grove and where it ends, continue along a track. At a junction of tracks and paths, keep ahead, in the Bottoms Lane direction, along another enclosed tarmac path to a stile. Climb it, walk along the left edge of a field and turn left through a gate. Turn right to continue along the right edge of a field and go through a gate onto a lane.

Turn right, at a public footpath sign to The Row and Railway Station turn left through a gate and walk along the right edge of a field. Just before reaching the field corner, turn right over a stile and head across a field to a gate. Go through, keep along the right edge of the next field and in the corner go through another gate and climb a stile onto a lane. Turn right, turn left through a gate, at a public footpath sign to Railway Station, and head downhill across a golf course – the route is well waymarked – to a stile.

Climb it and turn right along a road, passing Silverdale station. Take the first turning on the left, walk past the entrance to Leighton Moss Nature Reserve **(B)** and at a public bridleway sign to Leighton Hall Farm, turn right onto a track. This tree-lined track continues across a causeway between the lakes and marshes of the nature reserve, passing a public hide. Go through a gate on the far side and continue along the track, going through another gate, as far as a public footpath sign to Yealand Storrs.

At this point keep ahead to visit Leighton Hall **(C)**; otherwise turn left through a gate and follow a track across fields. After going through a gate, continue first along the right edge and then along the left edge of fields – passing through a succession of gates – to the point where the wall on the left turns left. Now keep ahead to join a wall on the right, go through a gate, continue along a track to the right of a house and bear right to go through one more gate onto a road.

Turn left to a fork, go through a gate, at a public footpath sign, and take the path ahead – bisecting the fork – through the woodland of Yealand Hall Allotment. Go through a gate and keep ahead to a fork, here continuing along the left-hand path to go through another gate. At a T-junction ahead, turn left onto an enclosed path and about 30 metres before the next gate, turn left through a gate and over a stile

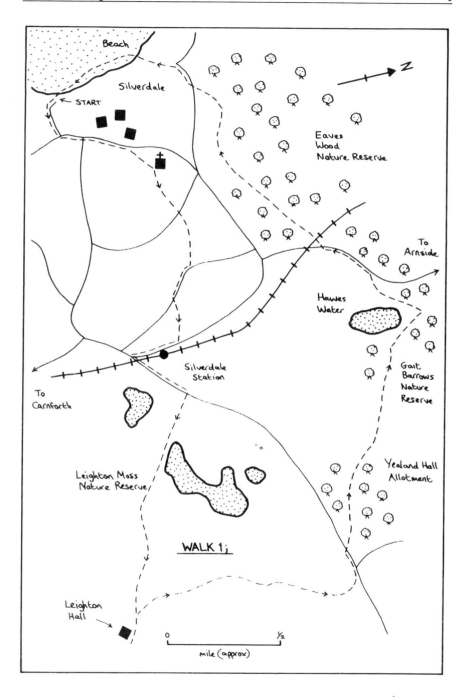

and head across a field corner. Turn right through a gate in a wall, here entering Gait Barrows Nature Reserve **(D)**,walk across a field, cross a low wall and continue to the far corner of the field. Climb a stile and walk along a path that curves left through woodland, by a wall on the left. Over to the left is Hawes Water.

Go through a gate onto a road, turn left and at a public footpath sign to Waterslack and Eaves Wood, turn right over a stile. Continue along a fence-lined path, which winds down to a gate. Go through it, turn left along a lane and at another footpath sign to Waterslack and Eaves Wood, turn right over a stile. Cross the railway line, climb a stile and keep ahead, crossing two tarmac drives, to climb another stile. Continue beside the Waterslack Garden Centre car park, cross another drive and climb a stile to enter Eaves Wood.

At a fork immediately ahead, take the left-hand path which heads uphill to a meeting of paths. Here continue along the left-hand path again and at the next fork in front of a wall gap, take the right-hand uphill path. Pass through a wall gap and continue ahead along a path which keeps close to the left inside-edge of the wood. At another fork take the left-hand path, following yellow waymarks, eventually descending to a tarmac track. Turn left, immediately turn right along a track, at a public footpath sign to Cove Road, and at a yellow waymark continue along a narrow, enclosed path – Wallings Lane – to a gate. Go through and walk along a track, between houses and bungalows, to join a lane.

Keep ahead and where the lane bends left, continue along another enclosed path to a road. Turn right and at a right bend, turn left along a lane – sign-posted 'The Shore, Cul de Sac and Footpath to Village' – which descends to a gate. Go through and continue along the shore, at the base of low limestone cliffs, to return to the start.

Features of Interest

(A) Until the 19th century, Silverdale was a remote, tiny and scattered hamlet on the shores of Morecambe Bay but its mild climate and favourable situation enabled it to develop into a small holiday resort, especially following the construction of the Furness railway. It makes an excellent walking centre, enjoying fine views across the bay and towards the Lakeland Fells, and with limestone outcrops and splendid woodlands in the immediate vicinity.

(B) The extensive and varied species of wildfowl and wading birds that are attracted to the reedbeds, woodland and shallow meres of the Leighton Moss Nature Reserve makes it hugely popular with birdwatchers. There is a shop, visitor centre, nature trails and a public hide.

(C) Originally a medieval manor house, Leighton Hall was rebuilt in the Gothic style in the mid 18th century and refaced in pale grey limestone in the early 19th century. Unlike many large houses, it has a pleasantly informal and lived-in atmosphere. It was the home of the Gillow family and, not unexpectedly, possesses many fine examples of Gillow furniture.

The setting, amidst sloping parkland and with imposing views of the Lakeland fells, is superb and there are attractive gardens. In the Aviary Garden is an unusual collection of birds of prey.

(D) The Gait Barrows National Nature Reserve was established in 1977 in order to protect one of the finest areas of limestone pavement in the country. The surrounding woods support a wide variety of wildlife and plants, with some ancient yew woodlands and important wetlands around Hawes Water.

2. Hornby and the River Lune

Start/Parking: Hornby – grid reference 584683.

Distance: 7 miles (11.3km).

Category: Moderate.

Refreshments: Castle and Royal Oak pubs at Hornby.

Terrain: Some field paths but most of the walk is across flat riverside meadows, muddy stretches are likely in places.

OS Maps: Landranger 97, Outdoor Leisure 41.

Public transport: Buses from Lancaster and Kirkby Lonsdale.

What you'll discover

This is a rather distorted figure-of-eight walk, with the outward and return halves briefly meeting at Loyn Bridge over the River Lune. Much of the route is across wide riverside meadows beside the Lune and Wenning and there are extensive views across the valley to the line of the Bowland Fells. Although Hornby Castle is not open to the public, its tower is in sight for much of the way and there are fine churches at Hornby and Gressingham.

Route Directions

Turn right out of the car park, follow the main road to the left and cross the bridge over the River Wenning. From here there is a fine view of Hornby Castle **(A)**. Continue through the village, passing the church **(B)** and after half a mile, bear left along a lane sign-posted to Gressingham. The lane descends below the earthworks of Castle Stede **(C)** on the right and curves left to cross Loyn Bridge over the River Lune. On the far side, turn right through a metal gate, immediately turn left over a stile and walk across a field. Climb a stile on the far side to rejoin the lane and continue along it into the small, quiet village of Gressingham. Turn left along a lane sign-posted to Eskrigge, passing in front of the church **(D)**, turn right at a T-junction and at a public footpath sign, turn left along the drive to Crowtrees. Pass in front of two houses to climb a ladder stile in a wall, keep ahead across grass, passing in front of another house, and climb a stile in a hedge.

Bear slightly right across a field, making for the right-hand corner, climb a stile just to the left of a tree and continue uphill across the next field, bearing right to climb another stile in the corner. Keep along the right edge of a field, go through a metal gate and continue along a track to a lane. Cross over, take the track ahead and on reaching a farm, go up steps on the left to climb a stile. Walk along the right edge of a field, passing in front of the farm, to another stile and climb that. Keep ahead to join a hedge and continue alongside it.

At a fence corner, keep straight ahead across the field to climb a stile,

The River Lune, near Hornby

turn left gently uphill along a track – this is a permissive route – and turn right in the field corner to continue along its top edge, by a hedge on the left. Climb a stile, continue along the right edge of the next field and now come impressive views to the left over the Lune valley, with both the confluence of the Lune and Wenning and tower of Hornby Castle clearly visible, and the line of the Bowland Fells on the horizon.

Descend to go through a metal gate and bear left to continue downhill to a stile. Climb it, keep ahead, passing to the left of farm buildings, and go through a gate onto a track. Turn left down the tree-lined track which bears right and at a public footpath sign, turn sharp left through a gate to join the well-waymarked Lune Valley Ramble. Continue down to the next public footpath sign, bear right across a meadow to a stile, climb it and turn left beside the River Lune.

Walk along the edge of wide riverside meadows, passing the confluence of the Lune and the Wenning, and after climbing a stile, continue along a tree-lined path, climbing two more stiles. The route then keeps along the bottom edge of sloping woodland and after crossing a footbridge over a stream, continues once more across meadows to Loyn Bridge. Climb a stone stile, turn right over the bridge and immediately turn left beside a metal gate, at a public footpath sign, and head down a track. Descend steps to the left of the track and turn sharp left to pass under the bridge.

If this path is flooded – which happens when the river is high – continue along the lane after crossing Loyn Bridge and at the side of a wooden bungalow, turn right over a stile and walk along the right edge of a field. Pass through a fence gap, steeply descend to the river and turn left to pick up the route.

After going under the bridge, climb a ladder stile, keep along the wooded riverbank, climb another stile to emerge from the trees and continue above the river. The path soon descends to keep beside the river – this part of the walk may well be muddy – and continues across meadows. Climb a ladder stile, follow the Lune to its meeting with the Wenning and turn left to walk beside the Wenning back to Hornby.

Climb a ladder stile, continue to the corner of the meadow, climb

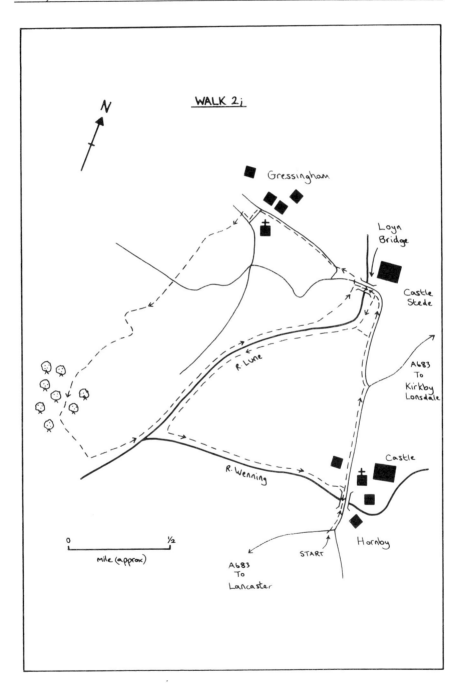

WALK 2i

N

Gressingham

Loyn
Bridge

Castle
Stede

R. Lune

A683
To
Kirkby
Lonsdale

R. Wenning

Castle

Hornby

0   ½

mile (approx)

START

A683
To
Lancaster

a stone stile and keep ahead along a path, which bends right to rejoin the river. Bear left along the tree-lined riverbank to Hornby Bridge, turning left in front of the bridge and then turning right through a gate onto the road. Turn right over the bridge to the start.

Features of Interest

(A) Hornby Castle occupies an imposing site above the River Wenning. It was originally a medieval pele tower, reconstructed in the 16th century, but the present castle dates mainly from the 19th century when it was extended for Pudsey Dawson, a wealthy financier. The castle is not open to the public.

(B) The church is dominated by its octagonal west tower, built by Edward Stanley, owner of the adjacent castle, in 1514, possibly as a thanksgiving for his safe return from the battle of Flodden the previous year. He was also responsible for the chancel but the rest of the church was rebuilt in the 19th century.

(C) The earthworks are all that remain of a Norman motte and bailey castle above the River Lune.

(D) The church at Gressingham has a particularly fine Norman south doorway but most of it was rebuilt in 1734.

3. Lancaster

Start: Castle Hill, in front of the Castle Gatehouse.

Parking: Lancaster.

Distance: 2 miles (3.2km).

Category: Easy.

Refreshments: Plenty of pubs, restaurants and tea and coffee shops in Lancaster

Terrain: Easy town walking.

Maps: Pick up a street map from the Tourist Information Centre on Castle Hill.

Public transport: Buses from all the surrounding towns; also Lancaster is on the main west coast rail line from London through Stafford, Crewe, Warrington, Wigan and Preston, and on to Carlisle and Glasgow.

What you'll discover

The walk enables you to appreciate the vital importance of Lancaster's geographical location on its historical development. Situated between hills and sea, at the lowest crossing point on the River Lune and commanding the main west coast route between England and Scotland, it is not surprising that both Roman invaders and later Norman conquerors established fortresses here. In the 18th century the river enabled Lancaster to enjoy a 'Golden Age' as a flourishing port and many fine Georgian buildings survive from that era of prosperity. However, the continual silting up of the Lune and distance from the main centres of commerce and industry in south Lancashire led to the town's relative decline in the 19th century, even losing its role as the county town to Preston. Thus it was spared some of the more unfortunate consequences of the Industrial Revolution and remains an essentially Georgian town, overlooked by a medieval castle and priory.

Route Directions

Keeping to the right of the castle, follow the walls round to the left and go up steps to walk between the castle on the left **(A)** and priory church **(B)** on the right.

Turn right along a path, sign-posted to the Maritime Museum, that heads downhill across fields. At a sign for Roman Bath House, a brief detour to the right leads to these ruins **(C)**. Return to the main path and continue downhill, crossing a footbridge and descending steps to St George's Quay. Turn left alongside the River Lune to the Customs House, now the Maritime Museum **(D)**. Retrace your steps along the quay, continue to the main road and turn right up China Street to the Judge's Lodgings **(E)**. Turn left along Church Street, turn left again into North Road and bear right to St John's Church. Turn right, turn left into Moor Lane and walk along it as far as the canal bridge. Here turn left to descend steps and turn right under the bridge to continue along the canal towpath **(F)**. Leave the canal at the second bridge, turn right along the road, turn right again and turn left into Dalton Square, dominated by the New Town Hall **(G)**. Turn right, then turn left along Gage Street, continue into the pedestrianised shopping area, turn right and left again along Market Street and walk into the Market Square. Passing to the left of the Old Town Hall **(H)** keep ahead, cross the main road and turn right up Castle Hill to the start.

Features of Interest

(A) Originally founded by Roger de Poitou in the late 11th century, Lancaster Castle has been enlarged and modernised many times and it is still in use as a law court and prison. The oldest parts are the massive Norman keep and the imposing gatehouse, the latter named after John of Gaunt but in fact built around 1400 by his son Henry IV. It was John of Gaunt, fourth son of Edward III, who began the link with the Crown. He married Blanche of Lancaster and their son deposed Richard II and ascended the throne as Henry IV in 1399, first of the Lancastrian kings. Since then all monarchs have held the title Duke of Lancaster.

The tour of the castle – inevitably restricted because part of it is still a prison and law court – includes the Shire Hall, added in the late 18th

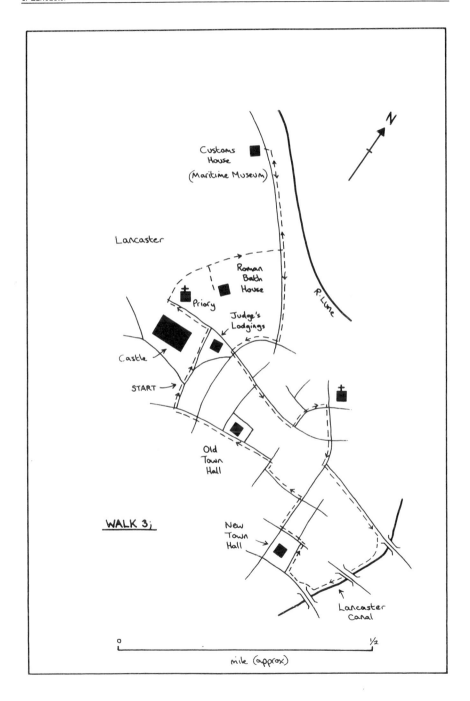

Customs House (Maritime Museum)

Lancaster

Roman Bath House

Priory

Judge's Lodgings

Castle

START

R. Lune

Old Town Hall

WALK 3;

New Town Hall

Lancaster Canal

0 ½

mile (approx)

century and noted for its vast collection of shields, dungeons and Drop Room. The latter, as the name indicates, is the room through which prisoners passed to their execution outside at Hanging Corner.

(B) The imposing, mainly 15th-century church that stands next to the castle was once part of a medieval priory, also founded by Roger de Poitou. During the Hundred Years' War, Henry V suppressed it because it was a dependency of a French abbey. It is particularly noted for the intricate carvings of the late medieval choir stalls. The west tower was rebuilt in the 18th century.

(C) Meagre they may be, but these are the only visible remains of Roman Lancaster. The bath house was part of a building that lay just outside the walls of the fort, demolished in the 4th century when the fort was rebuilt.

(D) The Customs House is the jewel in Lancaster's Georgian heritage. Built in 1764, it now houses an interesting Maritime Museum which covers the rise and fall of Lancaster as a port, and the history of the Lune estuary and Morecambe Bay.

(E) This well-proportioned 17th-century house is where the judges stayed while presiding over cases at the castle. It is now used as a Museum of Childhood and has a fine collection of furniture from the local Gillow firm.

(F) The Lancaster Canal was constructed in 1797 in an attempt to prolong the commercial prosperity of the town by providing a link with Preston and the more heavily populated south Lancashire. As you proceed along the towpath, the skyline on the left is dominated by the domed Ashton Memorial, built in 1909 by Lord Ashton, a local businessman, as a memorial to his wife. Also prominent is the tower and spire of the Roman Catholic cathedral, built around the middle of the 19th century and a fine example of the Victorian Gothic style.

(G) Lord Ashton was also responsible for the building of the New Town Hall in 1909.

(H) One of Lancaster's finest Georgian buildings, the Old Town Hall dates from the 1780s. It is now the City Museum.

4. Sunderland Point and Overton

Start/Parking: Middleton Sands, Beach car park — grid reference 413573.

Distance: 6½ miles (10.5km).

Category: Easy.

Refreshments: Ship and Globe pubs at Overton, Shippon Bar just before the end of the walk.

Terrain: A flat and easy to follow walk mostly over coastal marshes and across fields.

OS Maps: Landranger 102, Pathfinder 659.

Public transport: The walk could be started from Overton which is served by buses from Heysham and Morecambe.

What you'll discover

Apart from a modest climb to just over 100ft, this is an entirely flat walk over marshes and across fields on the north side of the Lune estuary. There are wide views throughout, extending across the estuary to the Fylde and Bowland Fells and on the other side of Morecambe Bay to the line of the Lakeland mountains. The route takes you across the coastal marshes to the tiny and isolated hamlet of Sunderland Point, once a busy port, and continues on to the village of Overton where a small Norman church overlooks the estuary.

Note that the road from Sunderland Point to Overton is sometimes flooded for several hours at high tide and it is important to check on the times of the tides by contacting Morecambe Tourist Information Centre (01524 582808/9).

Route Directions

Start by taking the track, at a public bridleway sign to Sunderland

Point, that leads off from the car park across the marshes. At a fork continue along the right-hand track and about 100 metres further on, turn left off the main track, at a blue-waymarked post, to walk along another track which keeps below the sea wall and a wire fence on the left.

Walk along this track as far as a public bridleway sign, which directs you to the left through a gate. At this point, keep ahead for a short distance to see Sambo's Grave **(A)**, looking out for some steps on the left which lead up to it. Return to the public bridleway sign, go through the gate and walk along a hedge-lined path which later widens into a track and continues into the hamlet of Sunderland Point **(B)**. Ahead are fine views across the Lune estuary to the line of the Bowland Fells, with the Ashton Memorial above Lancaster clearly visible. At the shore the route continues to the left and past the end of the hamlet you join the narrow causeway which winds across creeks and marshes to Overton.

Sambo's grave at Sunderland Point

At high tide this road is sometimes flooded and it is important to check on times with the local tourist information centre at Morecambe.

On approaching the end of the causeway, turn sharp right onto a track, at a public footpath sign to Chapel Lane via Bazil Point. At the next footpath sign, turn left over a ladder stile, in the Hall Greave direction, and

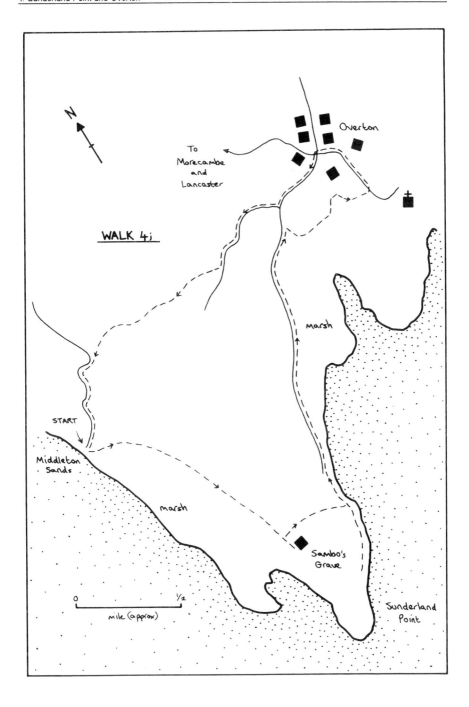

N

To
Morecambe
and
Lancaster

Overton

WALK 4i

marsh

START

Middleton
Sands

marsh

Sambo's
Grave

Sunderland
Point

0   ½
mile (approx)

head gently uphill across grass to the trig point at the top. Despite the modest height of this hill – just over 100ft (30m) – the all-round views are magnificent, embracing the estuary, Fylde coast, Bowland Fells, Lancaster, Morecambe Bay and the mountains of the Lake District.

Keep ahead past the trig point to a footpath sign, turn left, climb a ladder stile and walk along an enclosed path to a T-junction. Turn right onto an enclosed track, sign-posted to Chapel Lane, go through a kissing gate and keep ahead to a road. A short detour to the right and round a left bend brings you to Overton church **(C)**. Otherwise, the route continues to the left, following the road round left and right bends to a crossroads in the centre of Overton. Turn left to continue through the village and opposite the Globe, turn right along a lane, at a No Through Road sign.

Follow this winding lane as far as a public footpath sign to Carr Lane and Middleton where you turn right over a ladder stile. Walk across a field, making for the right edge of farm buildings in front, climb a ladder stile and keep ahead to climb another one at a crossroads of tracks and paths. Continue across a field to climb a stile and bear slightly right across the next field, making for a stile in the far right corner. After climbing it, keep along the left edge of a field, above a ditch on the left, following it as it curves right to a ladder stile in the field corner. Climb that, continue along the left edge of a field, climb another ladder stile and walk along a track, climbing one more ladder stile onto a lane.

Turn left and follow the lane around several bends back to the starting point.

Features of Interest

(A) Not much is known about Sambo but he was allegedly a Negro slave who died while accompanying his master, a cotton merchant, to England. As a heathen, he could not be buried in consecrated ground and therefore his grave lies by this remote and desolate shore. Take time to read the poignant verses inscribed on the grave.

(B) There is a pleasantly ghostly and melancholic air about

Sunderland Point and it is supremely difficult to visualise this tiny and remote hamlet as a busy and flourishing port, as it was in the early 18th century when cargoes of cotton, rum, tobacco and sugar were landed here from the American and Caribbean colonies. It was founded down here on the estuary by Robert Lawson, a local merchant, as a means of overcoming the problem of the silting up of the Lune which was threatening the prosperity of the port of Lancaster. Its remoteness and the continued silting up of the river ensured that it only enjoyed a brief heyday and by the end of the 18th century it had been largely superseded by Glasson Dock on the other side of the estuary. (See Walk 5)

Nowadays it comprises little more than two rows of cottages, mostly former warehouses, and a few larger houses. Outside one of the cottages stood the famous 'Cotton Tree', actually a female black poplar, but this succumbed to the gales of Christmas 1997 and finally fell down on New Years' Day 1998. At the south end of the hamlet the verandas and canopies of The Hall give the house something of the appearance of a plantation owners' residence from the Deep South.

(C) The attractive little church is about half a mile from the centre of the village, overlooking the estuary and directly opposite Glasson Dock. It is basically Norman, with a fine 12th-century south doorway. The chancel was built in the 18th century and the north transept, almost as long as the main body of the church, added in 1830.

Before the silting up of the Lune, Overton was a fishing and boat building village and some attractive old cottages survive in the village centre.

5. The Lune Estuary and Cockersand Abbey

Start/Parking: Conder Green picnic area – grid reference 457561.

Distance: 7 miles (11.3km).

Category: Moderate.

Refreshments: Stork pub at Conder Green, pubs and cafés at Glasson Dock.

Terrain: A flat walk mainly across reclaimed coastal marshes, with a brief opening section along the track of a disused railway and a middle stretch along the sea wall.

OS Maps: Landranger 102, Pathfinder 659.

Public transport: Infrequent bus service between Lancaster and Knott End.

What you'll discover

The first part of the walk follows a disused railway track into Glasson Dock where a branch of the Lancaster Canal joins the River Lune. You then cross reclaimed marshland to continue along the south side of the Lune estuary to the scanty and lonely remains of Cockersand Abbey. The final stage of the route heads inland across more fields reclaimed from former marshes. Throughout the walk there are extensive views across the flat landscape to the line of the Bowland fells, along the Fylde coast and across the Lune estuary and Morecambe Bay to the distant profile of the Lakeland mountains.

Route Directions

Turn left out of the car park to join the Lune Estuary Footpath, part of the Lancashire Coastal Way **(A)**. Cross a bridge over the River

Conder, go through a kissing gate and continue along an enclosed path. Go through another kissing gate, keep ahead – now parallel to the road – into Glasson Dock, turning left to the road at a Lancashire Coastal Way sign.

Turn right and take the first turning on the left to cross a bridge over the end of the canal basin **(B)**. Continue along Tithebarn Hill – the only hill on the walk – and at the top comes a superb view that includes the Lune estuary (with Sunderland Point and Heysham Power Station on the other side), Morecambe Bay and the Cumbrian mountains, the Fylde coast and the Bowland fells. A viewfinder on the left indicates all the wide-ranging places that can be seen from here on a clear day.

Keep along the road, which bears left, and at a left bend, turn right along a hedge-lined, tarmac track. The track – later it becomes a grassy track – continues to a gate. Go through it, and another, and keep by a line of low, widely-spaced trees on the right before curving left to a metal gate by a drainage channel. Go through that and keep ahead, going through two more gates and passing to the left of a farm, to reach the shore.

Turn left along a tarmac track above the shore of the Lune estuary. Past Lighthouse Cottage it becomes a rough track and after going through a kissing gate, continue along a narrow path, still above the shore, which bends left towards Cockersand Abbey. Go through another kissing gate and bear left off the Lancashire Coastal Way, passing to the right of the abbey ruins **(C)** and continuing to a stile in front of a deserted farmhouse. Climb it, follow a track to the right in front of the farm and then turn left through a metal gate. Continue along the track – ahead is a fine view of the Bowland fells – and climb a stile onto a lane at a bend.

Follow this lane around first a left bend, then a right bend, then another left bend and at a junction, turn right. Go round right and left bends again and about 300 metres after the lane bears left – just beyond a farmhouse – turn left over a stile, at a public footpath sign. Walk along the left edge of a field, go through a gate and keep ahead across the next field to another gate. Go through that one, continue along the left edge of the next two fields, going through another metal gate and picking up a definite track in the second field, to reach a T-junction to the right of a farm.

Turn right through a metal gate and at a fork immediately ahead, take the left-hand path, which keeps along the left edge of a field. Where the field edge starts to curve slightly right, go through a gate onto a tarmac track and turn right along it. After passing over a cattle-grid, turn right through a metal gate, at a public footpath sign, and continue along a track. Where the track bears slightly right into a field, keep ahead, between wire fences, and climb a stile to the left of a gate. Turn left along the left edge of a field, follow the field edge to the right and climb a stile in the corner onto a lane.

Turn left, follow the lane around a right bend and where it bends to the left, keep ahead across a footbridge, at a public footpath sign, and walk along the right edge of a field. Continue across two more footbridges and after the second one, turn right along the right field edge. Follow the field edge as it curves left, cut across a corner to pick up the field edge again and at the point where you are almost opposite the last footbridge that you crossed, turn right through a metal gate. Walk across a field to keep by a hedge on the right to another metal gate. Go through, continue along the right edge of the next field, by the hedge on the right, and go through a gate onto a road.

Turn left and cross first the canal bridge and then a bridge over the River Conder. In front of the Stork, turn left onto a lane, at a sign to Lune Estuary Coastal Path, to return to the start.

Features of Interest

(A) The Lune Estuary Footpath uses the track of a disused railway, built in 1883 to link Glasson Dock with the main line at Lancaster.

(B) Glasson Dock was established in 1787 in order to prolong the prosperity of the port of Lancaster which was being threatened by the continual silting up of the River Lune. An earlier attempt at Sunderland Point on the opposite side of the estuary (See Walk 4) had failed but Glasson Dock was scarcely more successful. The problem was not just the silting up of the river but the comparative

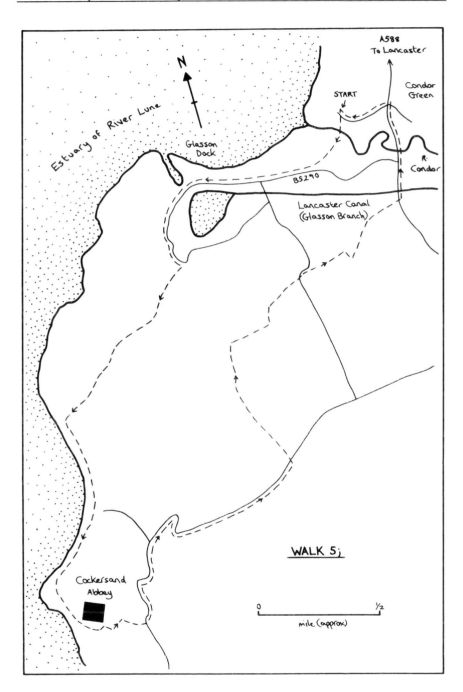

WALK 5;

0   ½

mile (approx)

distance of the Lancaster area from the main centres of industry and population in south Lancashire and the remoteness of both Glasson Dock and Sunderland Point. Several efforts were made to improve communications, notably the construction of the canal in 1826 to link the port with the main Lancaster Canal, and the building of the rail link in 1883. None of these worked and the Lune continued to decline as a commercial waterway.

Nowadays, Glasson Dock enjoys a new lease of life as a popular centre for pleasure boating and the canal basin is an attractive marina.

(C) Most medieval abbeys were built in fairly sheltered river valleys but Cockersand occupies a windswept site overlooking the sea and desolate coastal marshes. Little remains apart from a few crumbling walls and the 13th-century semi-octagonal chapter house. The latter survived because it became the burial place of the Catholic Dalton family of nearby Thurnham Hall after the abbey was dissolved in 1539.

Cockersand was originally founded as a hermitage in 1180 and became a Premonstratensian abbey shortly afterwards. Throughout the Middle Ages its monks played an important role in reclaiming the surrounding lands from the sea.

6. Slaidburn, Newton and the River Hodder

Start/Parking: Slaidburn — grid reference 714524.

Distance: 6 miles (9.7km).

Category: Moderate.

Refreshments: Riverbank Tea Room and Hark to Bounty at Slaidburn, Parkers Arms at Newton.

Terrain: Mainly across open country on the edge of the Bowland Fells, with a final stretch along a riverside path.

OS Maps: Landranger 103, Outdoor Leisure 41.

Public transport: Infrequent buses from Clitheroe and Settle, also Ribble Valley Rambler, Bowland Pathfinder and Bowland Rambler 'Leisure Links' bus services operate between Preston, Lancaster and Clitheroe on Sundays and Bank Holidays from May until September.

What you'll discover

This highly attractive walk, near the eastern fringes of the Forest of Bowland, begins in Slaidburn, once the administrative centre of the forest, and proceeds across mainly open country to the village of Newton, once a centre for Quaker worship. The final part of the route is along a beautiful riverside path beside the Hodder. There are outstanding views over the Hodder valley and Bowland Fells all the way.

Route Directions

Turn right out of the car park up through the village **(A)**, pass the Hark to Bounty and keep ahead along a lane. Just past the Slaidburn Health Centre, bear right through a wall gap, at a public footpath

Bridge over the River Hodder at Slaidburn

sign to Wood House, and follow a clear path through a lovely, steep-sided wooded valley beside Croasdale Brook.

Climb a stone stile; continue into more-open country and the path soon bears left away from the brook up to a stile. Climb it, head down to climb a ladder stile in the field corner, here rejoining Croasdale Brook, and continue beside it. After climbing a stone stile where the brook does a right bend, keep ahead to cross a footbridge over a tributary brook and continue across a field to a gate in the far corner.

Go through, walk along the right edge of a field, beside a wall, and follow that wall to the right to continue along a grassy track. Go through a gate into the farmyard of Myttons Farm Craft Centre and turn left along a walled track. On emerging from the walled section, turn left to climb a stile to the right of a barn and keep ahead to a stone stile in the left field corner. Climb that, continue along the right edge of the next field, follow the field edge to the left and then turn right, at a waymarked post.

Climb a stone stile in the field corner, bear slightly left along the

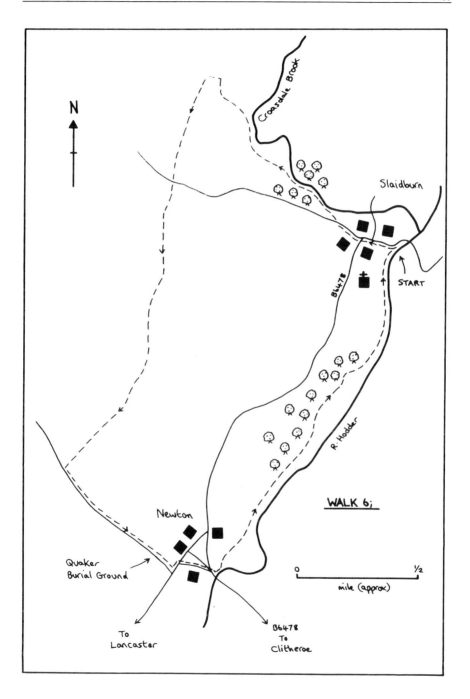

right edge of the next field, by a hedgebank on the right, and climb another stone stile just to the left of the field corner. In the next field bear slightly left away from the edge, making for a stile on the far side, and climb it onto a lane. Take the tarmac drive opposite to Parrock Head Farmhouse Hotel and Restaurant, pass in front of the hotel, turn left at the end of the building and go through a gate. Continue downhill across a field, in the direction of the farm seen ahead on the skyline, climb a stone stile and cross a footbridge over Eller Brook. Head up to Pain Hill Farm, making for a stone stile in the right-hand field corner, climb it and bear right to the corner of a barn.

Turn left and keep alongside a wall on the left to climb another stone stile. Keep ahead to join a wall and walk beside it towards the next farm. Climb a stone stile, keep ahead to go through a gate, continue along a track, passing to the right of the farm buildings, and follow it to a lane. Turn left steadily downhill into Newton, passing by a Quaker Burial Ground on the right and a former Quaker Meeting House **(B)** on the left. On the descent there is a grand view ahead of Waddington Fell across the Hodder valley.

At a T-junction turn left into the village, take the first turning on the right, sign-posted to Waddington and Clitheroe, and at another T-junction, turn right and walk down to the bridge over the River Hodder. In front of the bridge turn left through a gate, at a public footpath sign, keep ahead to go through another one, descend steps and continue along a riverside path. Cross a footbridge over a brook, keep ahead and look out for where you turn right to cross a brook and climb a stone stile. Turn left along the left edge of a meadow and climb a stile at the far narrow end of the meadow.

Continue below the steep slopes of Great Dunnow Wood and beside the river, go through a kissing gate, keep ahead, still below the wooded slopes, and bear slightly left to join a track. Walk along it and soon the tower of Slaidburn church comes into view. At a finger post keep ahead through a kissing gate and turn right over a stile, at a Riverside Path sign, to follow a permissive route back to Slaidburn.

Cross a footbridge and shortly climb a stile on the edge of a copse. Continue through the trees and climb another stile to emerge from them. Turn left onto a delightful riverside path and follow it, climbing two stiles and going through a kissing gate, to the start.

Features of Interest

(A) Slaidburn occupies a lovely position above the Hodder with a fine old bridge over the river. In the Middle Ages the village was the administrative centre of the Forest of Bowland and the forest courts met in what is now the Hark to Bounty Inn, where the court room is still preserved. Next to the mainly 15th-century church is the handsome facade of an early 18th-century grammar school building, founded by John Brennand and now forming part of the village primary school.

(B) Newton is also attractively situated above the River Hodder. The Quaker Burial Ground and Meeting House, both dating from the 18th century, are an indication of how the Quakers, as a result of their unorthodox and often unpopular views, were forced to seek out remote places like Newton at the time in order to avoid persecution. The former Meeting House is now a private cottage.

```
╔══════════════════════════════════════════════╗
║                                                ║
║   7. Whitewell and Browsholme Hall             ║
║                                                ║
╚══════════════════════════════════════════════╝
```

7. Whitewell and Browsholme Hall

Start: Whitewell – grid reference 659468.

Parking: In front of the church at Whitewell.

Distance: 7 miles (11.3km).

Category: Fairly strenuous.

Refreshments: The Inn at Whitewell.

Terrain: Several climbs and some rough moorland walking in places, paths not always visible on the ground and there will be muddy stretches after rain, some agility required.

OS Maps: Landranger 103, Outdoor Leisure 41.

Public transport: Infrequent buses from Clitheroe and Settle, also Ribble Valley Rambler and Bowland Pathfinder 'Leisure Links' bus services operate between Preston and Clitheroe on Sundays and Bank Holidays from May until September.

What you'll discover

You enjoy a succession of outstanding views over the Hodder valley and the surrounding fells on this walk near the southern edge of the Forest of Bowland. Possibly the most striking of these come near the end on the final descent into Whitewell. Historic interest is provided by the inn and small church at Whitewell at the start, and the 16th-century Browsholme Hall, passed at around the half-way point.

Route Directions

With your back to the church and hotel **(A)**, turn half-left and walk uphill along a lane. At a public footpath sign, turn right up steps and through a gate and keep ahead across a field. Pass between gateposts and continue up to reach a track in front of Seed Hill Farm.

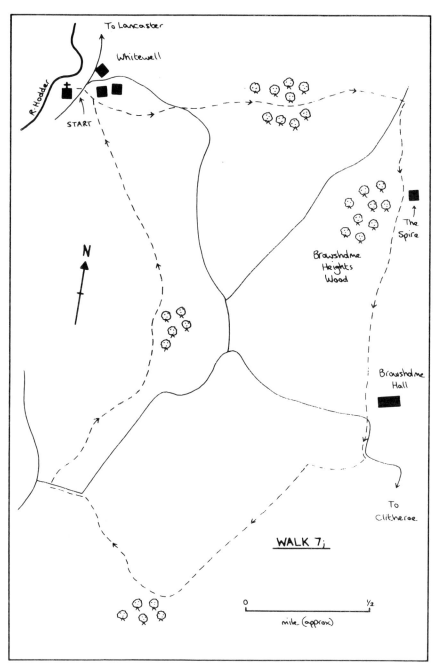

To Lancaster

Whitewell

R. Hodder

START

N

WALK 7;

Browsholme
Heights
Wood

The
Spire

Browsholme
Hall

To
Clitheroe

0   ½

mile (approx)

Turn left to pass to the right of the farmhouse and head uphill, alongside a line of trees and hedge-bank on the right, making for a gate. Go through, keep ahead along a grassy track for about 50 metres and bear left off it, continuing across the field and going through a gate to rejoin the lane. Cross over, go through the gate opposite and continue in the same direction to a ladder stile. Climb it and head across rough grassland, making for a circle of trees. Pass to the left of this circle and continue across towards the line of conifers ahead. Climb a ladder stile on the far side of the field, take the path through the conifer plantation and climb a stile to emerge from it.

Keep in the same direction across a field, cross a footbridge over a stream and go through two gates in fairly quick succession. Walk along the right edge of a field towards a farm, climb a stile and keep ahead to go through a gate. Pass between the farm buildings, continue along a tarmac track and go through a gate onto a lane.

Turn right and after a few metres, turn left over a stile and take an uphill path between conifers to a stile. Climb it, turn left beside the fence bordering the conifers on the left and at a fence corner, keep ahead across open grassland towards a battlemented tower (The Spire). Cross a track, keep ahead to climb a stile on the edge of woodland and walk along an enclosed path, passing to the right of The Spire **(B)**. Climb a stile, bear right along the edge of Browsholme Heights Wood and by a small brick building, bear left downhill, making for the right edge of a group of trees.

Bear left by a fence bordering the trees to a stile in the field corner. Climb it, turn right, climb another stile and continue across a field to a gate by the edge of woodland. Ahead is a superb view over the Hodder valley, with Longridge Fell on the skyline. Go through the gate, walk along a track, go through another gate and head gently downhill across a field to climb a stile onto a track. Follow the track down to a gate and go through to a T-junction. To the left is the car park for Browsholme Hall **(C)**; the route continues to the right to the road.

Keep ahead along the road and just after a left bend, turn right through a gate at a public footpath sign. Climb the embankment on the left and walk across a field to go through a gate onto a track. Turn right and follow the track as it bends left to Micklehurst Farm. Walk past the farm buildings, go through a gate, keep ahead across a field and go through another gate to join a track. Continue along it, going through a gate and on to Kinder Barn. Go through a gate to the left of the barn and keep along the right edge of a field to a stile. Climb it, turn right to ford a stream, go through a gate and bear left downhill across rough pasture. Continue more steeply downhill through trees and bear right alongside Cow Ark Brook.

Turn left to first climb a stile and then to cross a footbridge over the brook and head steeply up a wooded embankment. Cross a footbridge, continue up to climb a stile in front of a farmhouse and turn right to climb another. Walk along the track ahead by farm buildings and follow it to a road. Note that this track is not an official right of way but walkers are allowed to use it if they observe the Country Code and keep to the track.

Turn left at the road, follow it around a right bend and at a public footpath sign, turn right over a stile. Head downhill, bearing right away from a fence, to cross a footbridge over a stream, bear right and keep above the stream to a stile. Climb it, continue across a field, keeping roughly parallel to the stream, and look out for where you turn right over a half-hidden stile in the fence on the right by a holly bush. Continue above the stream, heading towards farm buildings, bear right to ford it and keep ahead to go through a gate onto a farm track. Walk along the track, passing to the right of Higher Lees Farm, and where it curves left, keep ahead across a field to a stile.

Climb it and bear slightly left across the next field, passing a solitary tree and continuing towards the woodland in front where you climb a stile at a wall corner. Keep by the wall bordering the woodland on the right, bearing right and later bearing left away from the trees towards Radholme Laund. Climb a stile, continue by the wall to the farm, turn right along a track, follow it to the left between farm buildings and keep ahead up to a gate. Go through, continue uphill along the right edge of a field and go through a kissing gate in the field corner. Bear right across the corner of the next field, go through another kissing gate and bear left to continue gently uphill along the left edge of a field.

Go through a gate and as you start to descend, a magnificent view unfolds over the Bowland Fells looking towards the Trough of

Bowland, with the sparkling River Hodder winding below. Just before reaching a wall corner, bear right to climb a stile and head steeply downhill to Seed Hill Farm. Here you pick up the outward route and retrace your steps to the start.

Features of Interest

(A) The small church and rambling old inn, standing side by side above the thickly-wooded banks of the River Hodder, make a picturesque grouping. The early 19th-century church occupies the site of an earlier chapel and parts of the inn, formerly a manor house, date back to the Middle Ages.

(B) The battlemented 'spire' on Browsholme Heights was a folly, built by the Parkers of Browsholme Hall as a landmark for people shooting on the estate.

(C) The hall has been owned and continuously occupied by the Parker family, for many centuries the hereditary wardens of the Forest of Bowland, since it was first built by Edmund Parker in the early 16th century. Despite a series of extensions and re-constructions in the 17th, 18th and early 19th centuries, it remains a fine example of a Tudor house with a handsome facade and impressive state rooms.

Browsholme Hall

---

8. Garstang and Calder Vale

Start/Parking: Garstang, High Street car park by the Discovery Centre — grid reference 493454.

Distance: 8½ miles (13.7km).

Category: Moderate.

Refreshments: Pubs and cafés at Garstang.

Terrain: Mainly flat walking along field paths, tracks and a canal towpath; likely to be muddy in places.

OS Maps: Landranger 102, Outdoor Leisure 41.

Public transport: Buses from Morecambe, Lancaster, Preston, Blackpool and Knott End.

What you'll discover

Despite some inevitable traffic noise from having to cross the M6 twice, this is a grand scenic walk in the countryside that lies between the flat expanses of the Fylde and the foothills of the Bowland Fells. There are a series of superb views of the western edge of the fells and across the Fylde to the coast, with both Blackpool Tower and Heysham Power Station visible on the horizon. In clear conditions the views extend across Morecambe Bay to the Cumbrian mountains. There is plenty of variety on a route that also includes attractive riverside and canalside walking, medieval castle ruins, an early 20th-century church in an isolated position, an equally isolated 19th-century mill and an impressive 18th-century aqueduct.

Route Directions

Facing the River Wyre, turn right along a tarmac riverside path and follow it to a road. Turn left to cross a bridge over the river and turn left again along Castle Lane.

The lane becomes a tarmac track which passes to the right of the ruins of Greenhalgh Castle **(A)** and continues to Castle Farm. Walk through the farmyard, keeping to the left of the farmhouse, and continue along a track to where it bends right. Here climb a stile and turn left along the left edge of a field which bears right. Ignore the first stile on the left but climb the second one, at a public footpath sign, and cross bridges over first a disused railway track, secondly the main London-Glasgow railway line, and finally the M6.

Continue along a left field edge, climb a stile and walk along a track which bears left, passing to the right of Parkhead Farm, and left again to a stile. Climb it, turn right along a track to a T-junction and turn right along a narrow, pleasant, tree-lined lane. After a quarter of a mile look out for a stile on the left which enables you to make a short detour to Barnacre church.

After climbing the stile, walk along the left edge of a field, by a stream on the left, turn left to cross a footbridge over the stream and climb another stile onto a track in front of farm buildings. Turn right, go through a gate and continue along the track to a stile. Climb it, keep along the right edge of a field, climb a stile and walk along an enclosed path to climb another stile and descend steps to a lane. Barnacre church **(B)** is just to the right. Retrace your steps to where you left the lane and turn left to continue along it. Where the lane bends left, keep ahead, at a public footpath sign, along a gently ascending concrete track. Before reaching a farm, turn left over a stile, continue through a wooded area and climb a stile in the top corner onto a track. Turn left, climb a stile, keep ahead over a ladder stile and continue uphill along the right edge of a field. After climbing a stone stile you continue along the right edge of a succession of fields, climbing several stiles, to emerge onto a road.

Turn right and almost immediately turn left over a stile, bear right to climb another and continue along the right edge of a field. After climbing another stile, bear left along an enclosed path, cross a footbridge and keep ahead across a field to climb a stile on the far side. Continue across the next field, climb a stile at the corner of a wood and walk along an enclosed path, by the left edge of the wood, eventually descending a flight of steps into Calder Vale **(C)**. Do not turn right along the road but take the lower, parallel tarmac track, passing

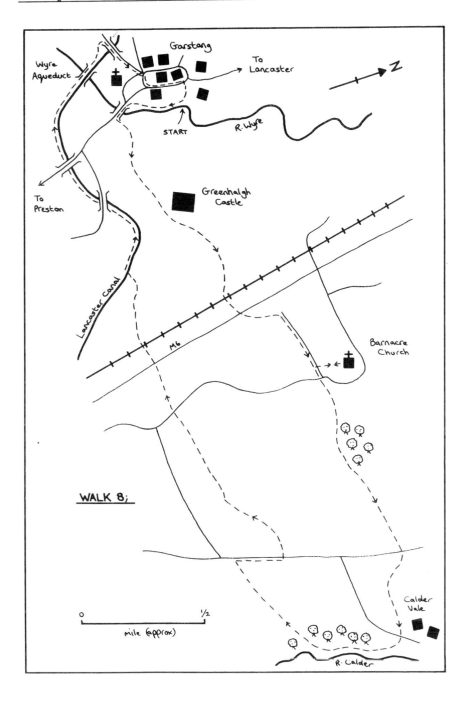

in front of cottages. This becomes a rough track, which continues through woodland along the right edge of the valley above the River Calder. Where the track bends left, turn right, at a public footpath sign to Sullom Side, and head uphill through the trees to a gate at the top edge of the woodland. Go through, continue along the left edge of a field, climb a stile and keep ahead along an enclosed, tree-lined and unusually wide track which descends to a stile. Climb it, continue towards a farm, go through a gate and keep ahead to a road.

Turn right and at a public footpath sign, turn left over a stile and walk along the right edge of a field alongside a ditch. Go through a gate, bear left and head gently downhill across a field towards a farm, going through another gate to the left of the main buildings. Keep ahead into the farmyard, turn left along a track, passing in front of the farmhouse, and just before reaching some trees, turn right through a gate. Walk along the left edge of a field, climb a stile and head downhill across the next field to climb a waymarked stile in front of farm buildings.

Turn right along a tarmac drive, follow it around a left bend and keep ahead to climb a stile. Walk along the left edge of a field, climb a stile in the corner and continue in the same direction as before along the right edge of a field. Climb another stile, keep along the right field edge and at the corner of a wood, turn right over a stile. Turn left, bear right away from the field edge and climb a stile onto a lane.

Continue along the track opposite, which leads to Bailton's Farm. Walk through the farmyard and the track bends first right and then left to recross the M6 and railway line. Where it curves left, turn right through a gate, walk across a field in the direction of the church tower seen in front, and climb a stile on the far side just beyond a solitary tree. Keep ahead across the next field, go through a gate and continue along the left edge of a field, curving left to join a track. Follow the track to the left and immediately after crossing a bridge over the Lancaster Canal, turn right over a stile and descend steps to the towpath **(D)**. Turn left and at the first bridge after crossing the Wyre Aqueduct **(E)** – number 62 – bear left up to a road. Turn right over the bridge and follow the road into Garstang, passing the 18th-century church. Keep ahead along Church Street into the Market Place **(F)**, bear left by the Market Cross, passing the Town Hall and walk along High Street to return to the start.

The Lancaster Canal near Garstang

Features of Interest

(A) There are two main reasons why, apart from a corner tower, there is little left of the castle built by the first Earl of Derby in 1490. First it was ordered to be destroyed by Oliver Cromwell after the Civil War in the late 1640s, and secondly the ruins were used by local farms, especially the adjacent Castle Farm, as a cheap source of building material.

(B) Despite the proximity of the motorway, there is a sense of isolation about Barnacre church. Built in 1905, it occupies an attractive position overlooking the flat country of the Fylde.

(C) You stumble almost unexpectedly upon the cotton mill and terraces of workers' cottages at Calder Vale, tucked away in a remote, steep-sided, wooded valley on the western slopes of the Forest of Bowland. The mill, established in 1835 by Richard and Jonathan Jackson, a Quaker family, made use of the water power provided by the fast-flowing River Calder.

(D) The Lancaster Canal was begun in 1792 and opened in 1797. It was built to link Lancaster with Preston and the main industrial areas of south Lancashire and runs through some outstandingly attractive countryside.

(E) This impressive single span aqueduct, built by John Rennie in 1797, carries the canal over the River Wyre. It is 110ft (33m) long and 34ft (10m) high.

(F) One of the attractive features of Garstang is the number of 'weinds' or alleyways that lead off from the High Street. The streets converge on the Market Place where both the Market Cross and nearby Town Hall date from the middle of the 18th century. The church is slightly later, built in 1770. Garstang's prosperity increased with the coming of the canal but declined following the construction of the Preston-Lancaster railway in the 1840s which bypassed the town.

9. Kirkham, Wesham and Wrea Green

Start: Kirkham, Market Place – grid reference 427323.

Parking: Kirkham.

Distance: 5½ miles (8.9km).

Category: Easy.

Refreshments: Pubs and cafés at Kirkham, pubs at Wesham, The Grapes pub at Wrea Green.

Terrain: Flat walking along roads, lanes, field paths and tracks; some of the paths and tracks are likely to be muddy, especially on the latter stages of the route.

OS Maps: Landranger 102, Pathfinders 678 and 679 .

Public transport: Buses from Preston, Blackpool, Lytham and St Annes; trains from Preston and Blackpool serve Kirkham and Wesham station.

What you'll discover

The walk starts in the market town of Kirkham and proceeds to the adjacent Wesham. The first part of the route involves some urban road walking but afterwards you head across fields to Wrea Green, an exceptionally attractive village with a spacious green complete with duck pond, thatched cottages, church and pub. Throughout the walk there are open and extensive views across the surrounding flat landscape of the Fylde.

Route Directions

From the Market Square **(A)** turn down Church Street and after passing to the left of the church, the route continues along a tarmac track.

Where the track turns right to Carr Farm, keep ahead over a stile and continue along a track to climb another one. Cross a stream, keep ahead, by a wire fence on the right, pass under a railway bridge and climb a stile.

Walk across the field ahead to a stile, climb it and head gently uphill along the right edge of a field. Do not climb the next stile but turn left along the top edge of the field, by a wire fence on the right, and before reaching the field corner, bear left across to a stile on the edge of houses. Climb it, walk along a path and continue along a road (Derby Road), passing Wesham Hospital across the green to the right. At a crossroads in Wesham **(B)**, keep ahead along Billington Street East, take the first turning on the left, turn right along Market Street and follow it to the end.

Keep ahead along a tarmac path, turn left along another tarmac path, at a public footpath sign, and cross a railway bridge. Where the path ends, cross a road, turn right, at another public footpath sign, and walk across a field, veering right away from the field edge and making for steps at the foot of the embankment in front. Climb them, cross a road, descend steps on the other side and bear slightly left to follow a path across a field towards trees. Cross a footbridge over Wrongway Brook, keep ahead over a stile and continue along the left edge of the next two fields. In the corner of the second field, climb a stile and keep ahead through a gate to a road.

Cross over, turn left and where the tarmac path forks, take the right-hand path which curves right to continue along the road towards Wrea Green. At a public footpath sign, turn right over a stile and walk across a field, continuing along the right edge of a copse to a stile. Climb it, keep ahead by a hedge on the right, climb a stile and continue, now by a hedge on the left, to climb another stile. Keep ahead along an enclosed, hedge-lined path, climb a stile and continue across a field, bearing slightly left to a ladder stile.

Climb that, turn left for a few metres, turn right to cross the railway line carefully, climb another ladder stile and walk across the next field, looking out for a stile beside a gate. Climb it and continue in the same direction across the next field, making for a group of trees in front of a house. Climb a stile, turn right along a drive to the road at Fox Lane Ends and turn left, re-crossing the railway, into

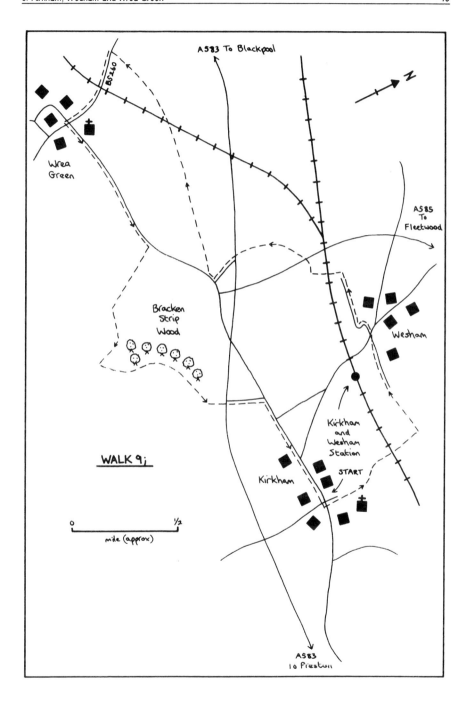

Wrea Green (C). At a crossroads by the village green, turn left along Ribby Road, passing the church, and after three-quarters of a mile – just before the road bears left – turn right along a tarmac track (Browns Lane). Follow this track for three-quarters of a mile and just after passing farm buildings – and a few metres after the track bends right – look out for a gate on the left. Facing it, turn left to climb a rather indistinct stile and head gently uphill across a field, keeping well to the left of a pond and making for a stile in front of a barn and to the left of a house.

Climb it – and another immediately in front – keep to the left of the farm buildings and climb another stile. Walk along the left edge of a paddock, by a narrow strip of woodland (Bracken Strip Wood) on the left, climb a stile and continue along the left edge of the next field. Climb a stile in the field corner, follow a path through trees and scrub, climb another stile and keep along the right edge of a field. After climbing the next stile, turn left along a track to the Kirkham bypass.

Cross over, walk along the road opposite and, at a crossroads, turn right. Follow the road back to the centre of Kirkham, heading gently up Poulton Street to return to the Market Square.

The picturesque village of Wrea Green

Features of Interest

(A) There has been a market at Kirkham since 1296 and the most striking feature of the Market Square is the fish stones grouped around a restored Victorian street lamp. These date from 1829 and local fishmongers used to sell their produce from them. The church was founded in Anglo-Saxon times but was mostly rebuilt in 1822. The imposing tower and spire, 150ft (45m) high, was added about 20 years later.

(B) The adjoining industrial town of Wesham developed in the 1840s following the construction of the railway.

(C) Wrea Green – full name Ribby-with-Wrea – is one of the most attractive villages in the Fylde and the views looking across the spacious green to the tower and spire of the church, especially from the duck pond in the north west corner, are idyllic. The church was built in 1848-9. On summer weekends the scene is further enhanced when a cricket match is taking place on the green.

10. Ribchester and the River Ribble

Start/Parking: Ribchester – grid reference 650353.

Distance: 6 miles (9.7km).

Category: Moderate.

Refreshments: Pubs and tea shop at Ribchester.

Terrain: A gently undulating route with pleasant riverside walking and some good wooded stretches, mostly on clear farm tracks and field paths.

OS Maps: Landranger 103, Explorer 19.

Public transport: Buses from Preston and Blackburn.

What you'll discover

On this walk, amidst some of the finest scenery in the Ribble valley, you start by Lancashire's principal Roman remains and pass a former monastic church and 18th-century almshouses. There is some lovely walking by the river, using the well-waymarked Ribble Way, several areas of attractive woodland and grand views over the valley to the unmistakable outline of Pendle Hill.

Route Directions

Turn right out of the car park and walk through the village to the river. The entrance to the Roman Museum **(A)** is to the right but the route turns left onto a tarmac path above the river, here joining the Ribble Way. The path curves left away from the river alongside a stream, passes the entrance to the Roman Bath House **(B)** and continues to a road.

Turn right, turn right again at a T-junction and follow the road for

The Almshouses at Stydd

three-quarters of a mile to Ribchester Bridge. Where the road turns right over the bridge, keep ahead along a track beside the river. At Dewhurst House Farm, keep ahead into the farmyard and turn right, at a Ribble Way sign, along a path to a ladder stile. Climb it, turn left alongside the Ribble again and the path later skirts the right edge of woodland and bears right down to a stile. After climbing it, cross a footbridge and continue along a winding path through Haugh Wood, following the river round a right bend.

Look out for where a footpath sign directs you to bear left away from the river to a stile. Climb it, turn left to head up a grassy bank and keep ahead across a field. Over a slight brow a grand view unfolds ahead along the Ribble, with Pendle Hill in the background. Descend to climb a ladder stile on the far side of the field, bear left and head uphill across the next field, making for a stile in the top corner. Climb it, continue in the same direction, go through a gate and turn left along a tarmac track. Go through another gate and walk on through a farmyard. Continue along the track, which later keeps along the left edge of Clough Bank Wood, as far as Grindlestone House Farm.

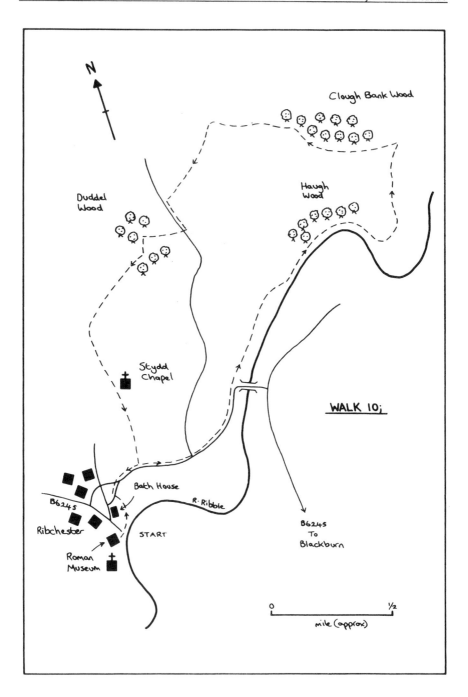

Here turn left through the farmyard, climb a stile, walk along the right edge of a field and climb another stile into the next field. Keep ahead for about 20 metres and then climb two stiles in quick succession and continue along the left edge of the next three fields, passing through a gap and climbing another stile. On the edge of a depression near the end of the third field, turn left over a stile and follow the rim of the depression to the right, descending to climb a stile onto a lane.

Turn left downhill and, at a public footpath sign, turn right along a track, passing in front of Dutton Hall. Just before the track curves right, turn left through a waymarked gate, walk along the top edge of a field and climb a stile beside a circular metal tank. Continue along the top right edge of the next field towards Duddel Wood, climb a stile and bear right to follow a path down through the wood to the banks of Duddel Brook. Turn left alongside the brook, turn right to cross a footbridge over it and take the path ahead up through the trees to a stile on the edge of the wood.

Bear left across a field and keep along its left edge to a stile in the field corner. Climb it, continue in the same direction across the next field, skirting a hedge corner and making for a stile on the far side. Climb it, follow a track down to a farm and walk through the farmyard, negotiating several gates. Continue along the track, passing Stydd Chapel **(C)**, turn right over a bridge and walk past the Stydd Almshouses **(D)** to the road.

Here you rejoin the outward route and retrace your steps to the start.

Features of Interest

(A) The museum occupies part of the site of the Roman fort of Bremetennacum, built around 78 AD. Very little exists above ground; some lies under the river, as the Ribble has changed course since Roman times, and part is below the medieval church. Many of the items excavated from the fort are on display in the museum but the only visible structure is the granary with its hypocaust, or underfloor heating system. The fort lay on the important north-south route between Hadrian's Wall and Manchester, and on the east-west route to the forts at Ilkley and York.

(B) The Bath House lay just outside the walls of the fort and was in use between about 100 and 225 AD. Both civilians and soldiers used its facilities. Part of it remains unexcavated beneath the adjacent school and playground.

(C) This isolated church, parts of which date back to the 12th century, belonged to a small monastery or commandery of the Knights Hospitallers of St John of Jerusalem, a crusading order. It was dissolved around 1338.

(D) These unusually handsome almshouses were built in the early 18th century by the Shireburns of Stonyhurst to house five poor people.

11. Stonyhurst and the Three Rivers

Start: Hurst Green – grid reference 685379.

Parking: Roadside parking in Hurst Green

Distance: 7 miles (11.3km).

Category: Moderate..

Refreshments: Several pubs at Hurst Green.

Terrain: Mostly easy riverside walking with just a few modest climbs.

OS Maps: Landranger 103, Explorer 19.

Public transport: Buses from Clitheroe and Longridge.

What you'll discover

"The Hodder, the Calder, Ribble and rain, All meet together, in Mitton domain" according to a local saying. On this walk, you meet the first three of these; hopefully you will avoid the fourth. Starting at the village of Hurst Green on the north side of the Ribble valley, the route passes by Stonyhurst College and then descends to the River Hodder. Most of the rest of the way is a splendid riverside stroll along the banks of first the Hodder and later the Ribble.

Route Directions

With your back to the Shireburn Arms, walk along Avenue Road and after passing the Shireburn Almshouses **(A)**, turn right along a tarmac track (Smithy Row). At the end of a line of cottages, keep ahead along an enclosed path which bends left, turn right through a kissing gate and continue along the left edge of fields, going through several kissing gates. The path curves left, descends to cross a stream and continues uphill, by the right edge of woodland, to a gate.

Go through and walk along a track which passes in front of Stonyhurst College **(B)** and continues to a road. Turn right and a few metres after passing Stonyhurst post office, turn left onto a tarmac track between houses. The track degenerates into a rough track and continues across fields. Where it bends left, keep ahead, at a yellow waymark, to climb a stile and walk along the left edge of a field bordering woodland. Climb a stile and keep in the same direction along the top edge of the wood, later descending steeply, via steps, through the trees to a footbridge. Cross it and keep ahead to the Hodder.

Turn right and the path first heads uphill above the river, passes by a large house and then descends to a kissing gate. Go through and follow the river around a right bend, going through several more kissing gates, to reach the road by Lower Hodder Bridge. Ahead is the picturesque Old Bridge or Cromwell's Bridge **(C)**.

Turn right uphill along the road and opposite a bus shelter, turn left over a ladder stile and walk along the right edge of a field. The rest of the walk follows the well-waymarked Ribble Way. Climb a stile, continue uphill to climb another and keep along the left edge of a field that borders steeply sloping woodland. After following the field edge to the right, look out for where you turn left through a kissing gate and walk across a field in the direction of a large house, Winckley Hall. Go through another kissing gate on the far side of the field and turn left along a track which passes the hall and descends to a farm.

Walk between the farm buildings, turn right to rejoin the Hodder and keep alongside it to Hodder Foot, the meeting of the Hodder and Ribble. Continue by the Ribble to Calder Foot, the confluence of the Ribble and Calder, and then veer away from the river towards an abandoned building. Head across meadows, go through a kissing gate and keep beside the Ribble again, passing Jumbles Rocks. Follow the river around a left bend – there are several stiles on this section – climb a stile by an aqueduct and continue towards woodland, bearing slightly right away from the river.

Climb a stile, cross a footbridge over a stream and head up through trees to climb a stile at the top end of the wood. Keep along the left edge of woodland, bear right to cross a plank footbridge and climb a stile. Head gently uphill along a low ridge between ditches

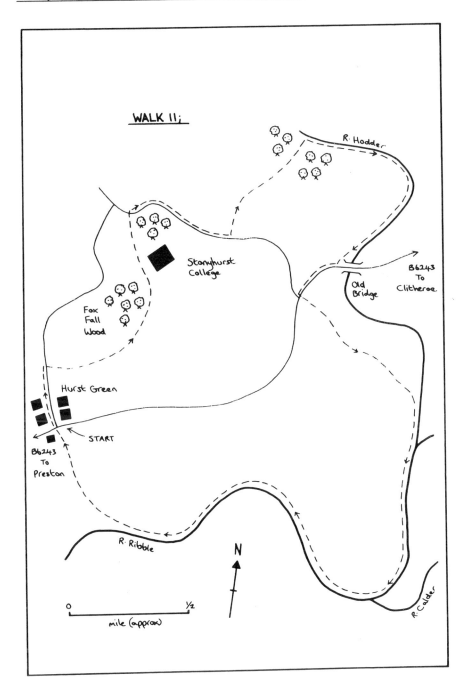

WALK II;

R. Hodder

Stonyhurst College

Fox Fall Wood

B6243 To Clitheroe

Old Bridge

Hurst Green

START

B6243 To Preston

R. Ribble

N

R. Calder

0   ½
mile (approx)

and turn right to cross a ditch. Turn left, continue uphill and climb a stone stile in the top corner of the field. Keep ahead by the side of the Shireburn Arms to return to the start.

Cromwell's Bridge over the River Hodder

Features of Interest

(A) The almshouses, built in 1706, originally stood at Kemple End and were moved to their present site just after the Second World War.

(B) Stonyhurst has certainly had a varied history. It was originally an Elizabethan mansion, started in 1592 by Sir Richard Shireburn, an ambitious man who largely embraced the Protestant Church of England for political advantage. Later members of the family reverted to the Catholic faith, which made them the objects of intense suspicion at a time when Catholics were often considered to be enemy agents in the service of the kings of Spain or France. During the Civil War that arch anti-Catholic Oliver Cromwell is alleged to have slept here, protected by pistols at the ready and armed guards around him.

After the male line of the Shireburns died out in the 18th century, the house passed by marriage to the Welds who neglected it in favour of their main residence at Lulworth in Dorset. Stonyhurst became derelict but during the anti-Catholic fervour of the French Revolution, Thomas Weld offered it to the expelled Jesuits. They accepted, restored and considerably extended the house, adding the chapel in 1830, and established a college. Thus Stonyhurst took on a new lease of life as an educational establishment, a role it still enjoys today as one of the principal Roman Catholic public schools in the country.

(C) This ancient bridge is usually called Cromwell's Bridge because Cromwell's troops are alleged to have crossed the river here in 1648 on their way to the battle of Preston.

12. Whalley and the Calder Valley

Start/Parking: Spring Wood picnic site – grid reference 742361.

Distance: 6½ miles (10.5km).

Category: Moderate.

Refreshments: Gamecock Inn near Cock Bridge, pubs and cafés at Whalley, Cloisters Coffee Shop at Whalley Abbey.

Terrain: There are indistinct paths is places – some of them likely to be muddy – and several moderate climbs.

OS Maps: Landranger 103, Explorer 19.

Public transport: The walk could be started from Whalley which is served by buses from Clitheroe, Blackburn, Accrington and Burnley, and by trains from Clitheroe and Blackburn.

What you'll discover

This grand scenic walk provides a series of outstanding views over the Calder valley. There is also the opportunity to explore the interesting and historic village of Whalley, dominated by an imposing Victorian railway viaduct and possessing both a ruined abbey and a medieval church with three ancient crosses in the churchyard.

Route Directions

Turn left out of the car park along the main road and at a public footpath sign, turn left through a wall gap and head steadily uphill along the left edge of Whalley golf course, with Spring Wood on your left. Cross a footbridge on the left just beyond the top edge of the wood and walk across a field, later heading uphill by a fence on the left to climb a stile in the top corner. Climb two more stiles, keep by a wall on the right, passing the buildings of Clerk Hill, and turn right along a track to a tarmac drive.

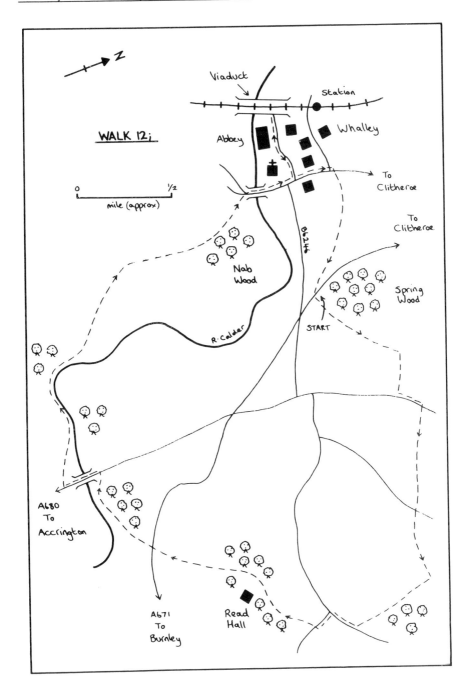

Turn left to a lane, turn left again and turn right along the second of two parallel farm drives – the one to Hollins Farm. Go through a gate to the left of the farm buildings, now a riding stables, keep ahead over a stream to go through another gate, and turn right head downhill along the right edge of a field, curving left to reach a road. Go through a wall gap opposite, pass through a gate into the next field, bear left across it and near the bottom corner – where the field narrows – climb a stile in a wall.

Keep ahead, turn right to cross a footbridge over Sabden Brook and head uphill to enter Hodgeon Stone Plantation. On emerging from the trees, walk along an enclosed track to a tarmac drive by another riding centre and continue along the track to a road. Turn right, at a T-junction turn left, in the Read direction, and opposite a bench turn right over a stile and bear left across a field. On the far side turn right onto a tarmac drive, follow it around the back of Read Hall **(A)** and continue through the park to reach the A671 by a lodge.

Take the track opposite, which descends to Read Garden Centre. To the left the scene is dominated by the disused Martholme Viaduct **(B)**. Walk along a track beside the River Calder up to the A680, turn left over Cock Bridge and just before the Gamecock, turn right over a stile. The path gradually descends to the riverbank, keeps alongside it and at a bend climbs above the river. The views from here over the valley are superb. Turn right over a ladder stile and continue through trees, later descending steeply, via steps, to a stile.

Climb it, cross a footbridge, walk across a field, negotiate another footbridge and stile and continue along the bottom right edge of a field. Turn right over the next stile, head uphill, climb a stile in the top corner of the field and continue along an enclosed path – later a tarmac track – to a junction.

Bear right along Dean Lane, which becomes a rough track, and soon after passing to the left of a large house (Whalley Banks) bear right onto a path, at a public bridleway sign. The path descends quite steeply through Nab Wood and divides into two parallel paths – bridleway on the left and footpath on the right. From the footpath you get the best views over the Calder valley, Whalley and the great viaduct to the west of the village **(C)**. At a lane turn right down to Whalley Bridge, turn right over it and walk through the village. A brief detour to the left along Church Street leads to the church **(D)** and abbey ruins **(E)**.

Opposite Station Road, turn right along Brookes Lane and, after the lane ends, bear right through a gate. Walk along a track and, in front of a gate, bear right to climb a stile. Head steadily uphill across a field and at the top end, climb another stile and continue to emerge onto the main road opposite Spring Wood picnic site.

Whalley Abbey

Features of Interest

(A) There has been a manor house on this site since the Middle Ages but the present Read Hall was rebuilt in the early 19th century.

(B) The 19th-century Martholme Viaduct was built to carry the railway across the Calder valley.

(C) The brick-built viaduct that spans the Calder valley, a triumph of Victorian engineering, was constructed around the middle of the 19th century. It is 2037ft (617m) long and has 49 arches.

(D) Although there has been a place of worship on the site since Anglo-Saxon times, the church dates mainly from the 13th century. It is particularly noted for the magnificent 15th-century choir stalls, taken from the nearby abbey after the dissolution. In the churchyard are three carved crosses which date from somewhere between the 9th and 11th centuries. They are thought to be Celtic but may possibly have Anglian and Viking influences.

(E) Whalley Abbey was founded in 1283 by Cistercian monks who moved here from Stanlow on the River Mersey because the site there was liable to flooding. The most impressive features are the two gatehouses. Visitors enter by the north east gatehouse, completed around 1480, and a little further along the road and beyond the abbey precincts is the vaulted, 14th-century north west gatehouse. Most of the surviving buildings date from the 14th century and although there is nothing left of the church apart from foundations, substantial parts of the cloisters and domestic buildings remain.

Henry VIII dissolved the abbey in 1536 and the last abbot, John Paslew, was hanged at Lancaster Castle in the following year for being involved in the Pilgrimage of Grace, a rebellion against the closure of the monasteries. After the Dissolution, the abbey buildings and land were bought by the Assheton family, who built a mansion on the site of the abbot's house and infirmary. This Elizabethan house now serves as a conference centre for the diocese of Blackburn.

13. Clitheroe and Mitton

Start: Clitheroe, Market Place – grid reference 744419.

Parking: Clitheroe.

Distance: 9 miles (14.5km).

Category: Moderate.

Refreshments: Pubs and cafés at Clitheroe; Mitton Hall (which comprises Owd Ned's Tavern and the Old Stonehouse Restaurant), Aspinall Arms, Three Fishes and Hillcrest Tea Rooms at Mitton; Riverside Café (seasonal opening) and Edisford Bridge at Edisford Bridge.

Terrain: Fairly level walking mostly along quiet lanes, farm tracks and field and riverside paths. Muddy conditions are likely in places, especially on the first half of the route to Mitton.

OS Maps: Landranger 103, Outdoor Leisure 41.

Public transport: Buses from Skipton, Burnley, Accrington, Blackburn, Preston and Manchester; trains from Blackburn and Manchester.

What you'll discover

Historic interest and grand views are in abundance on this lengthy but undemanding walk that starts from the capital of the Ribble valley. The historic interest is provided by the Norman castle at Clitheroe, a section of Roman road, the 16th-century Mitton Hall, the medieval church at Mitton and the 19th-century industrial community at Low Moor on the edge of Clitheroe. Throughout the walk there are a succession of fine views along the Ribble and across the valley to Kemple End and Pendle Hill, especially from the Ribble Way, and the church tower and castle at Clitheroe are seen from different angles at many points on the route.

Route Directions

Start in the Market Place and, with your back to the library and facing the castle **(A)**, turn left down Wellgate. Keep ahead along Shawbridge Street to a T-junction, turn right and almost immediately turn left to continue along Shawbridge Street. Turn right along Hayhurst Street – which becomes Littlemoor Road – and after half a mile, turn left onto an enclosed path, at a public footpath sign to Pendleton.

Turn right at a road and after a few metres, turn left, at a public footpath sign, along another enclosed path. The path curves right to keep along the right edge of a playing field and bends left to reach a stile. Climb it, walk across a field, cross a footbridge over a stream and head across the next field towards the corner of a wood. At the corner descend, by a wall on the left, to cross a footbridge over a stream, head up again and where the low wall on the left ends, go through a kissing gate.

Walk along a track, which curves left and continues to a lane. Turn right along the lane for three-quarters of a mile to emerge, via a gate, onto a road. Turn right and at a public footpath sign, turn left over a ladder stile and walk across a field to a stile. Climb it, keep along the right edge of a field and in the corner climb another stile and turn left onto a tarmac drive. Where the drive bears right, keep

The Norman keep of Clitheroe Castle

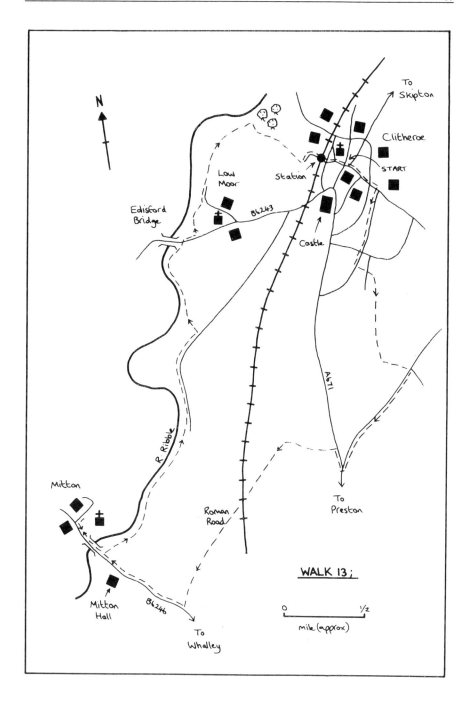

N

To
Skipton

Clitheroe

START

Low
Moor

Station

Edisford
Bridge

B6243

Castle

A671

R. Ribble

Mitton

Roman
Road

To
Preston

WALK 13;

Mitton
Hall

B6246

To
Whalley

0   ½

mile (approx)

ahead into a farmyard, veer left to pass to the left of a barn, go through a gate, turn right around the end of the barn and turn left over a stile to continue along a track.

This pleasant, broad, tree- and hedge-lined track, which is on the line of a Roman road **(B)**, leads to a railway line. Cross it carefully. continue along the right edge of a field, by a line of trees, climb a ladder stile and keep along the right edge of the next field. Where the field edge bends right, keep straight ahead, passing the base of an old cross and drawing closer to the right field edge again. Ford a stream, bear slightly left away from the field edge and head across rough pasture. There is no clear path at this point but on the far side look out for some stepping-stones over Barrow Brook.

Cross the stepping-stones, turn right to climb a stile and the way continues above the right edge of a sunken track to emerge, via a gate, onto a road. Turn right and follow the road into Mitton, passing Little Mitton Hall **(C)**, crossing Mitton Bridge – there is a superb view from here along the Ribble with Pendle Hill in the background – and heading up into the small village. The church **(D)** is along the first lane on the right.

Retrace your steps over Mitton Bridge and just beyond the Aspinall Arms, turn left through a kissing gate to join the Ribble Way. Most of the remainder of the route follows this well-waymarked trail. Bear slightly right uphill, rejoining the field edge at the top and continuing to a stile in the corner. Climb it, keep ahead along the left edge of a field high above the river and the field edge curves right to a kissing gate. Go through, keep ahead to cross a footbridge over a stream and continue diagonally across a meadow to reach the river by a weir. Bear right along a track beside the Ribble, passing an aqueduct, and continue to a farm.

Climb a stile, walk through the farmyard, turn right at the corner of a barn and turn left along a track. The track soon becomes a tarmac lane and you follow it as far as public footpath and Ribble Way signs just after crossing a bridge over a stream. Turn left here along a track, take the first track on the right and immediately go through a kissing gate. Walk diagonally across a field, go through another gate and the path descends to rejoin the riverbank. Go through a kissing gate and continue beside the Ribble, going through another kissing gate and passing through the Edisford recreation area, to Edisford Bridge.

In front of the bridge bear right up to the road and at a sign 'Swimming Pool', turn left along the drive to Ribblesdale Pool. Where the drive ends, keep ahead across grass to a Ribble Way post and turn right along the left edge of a playing field above the river. Look out for where the next Ribble Way post directs you to bear right across the field corner and pass in front of houses to reach a road at Low Moor **(E)**. Turn left, almost immediately turn right and at a fork take the right-hand road. The road becomes a track and you keep along it as far as a kissing gate and Ribble Way sign.

Go through the kissing gate and follow the path towards the river, taking care not to descend to the riverbank but bearing right to keep along the embankment above it. The elegant facade seen on the other side of the Ribble is Waddow Hall, owned by the Girl Guide Association. At the point where the path starts to descend into trees, turn right and walk across the field to go through a kissing gate in the corner. Continue along the left edge of a field to a pair of kissing gates, go through the right-hand one and keep ahead across the next field to a stile. Climb it, continue across a field and climb another stile onto a lane (Back Commons).

Turn left, then turn right along Kirkmoor Road and where the road bends right, turn left towards the railway station. Take the tarmac path that passes between the station and houses, turn right under a railway bridge and turn right again. In front of the station entrance turn left, follow the road uphill to a crossroads and turn left to the start.

Features of Interest

(A) Although the Norman keep of Clitheroe Castle claims to be the smallest in the country, it still dominates the town and surrounding area from its abrupt limestone hill. Built in the early 12th century, it is the only surviving part of the medieval castle of the de Lacys, who owned extensive estates in Lancashire. The other buildings nearby are later re-constructions and one of them houses the Castle Museum. This is mainly devoted to the history and geology of Clitheroe and the Ribble valley. The town it overlooks is one of the oldest boroughs in Lancashire, with a charter dating back to 1147. On the opposite – and smaller – hill stands the church, founded in 1122 but mostly rebuilt in 1828-9. The top stage of the tower and spire were added in 1844.

(B) The line of this Roman road can be traced on the Ordnance Survey maps. It ran between the forts at Ribchester and Ilkley.

(C) Mitton was divided into two by the Ribble and until the boundary changes of 1974, Little Mitton was in Lancashire and Great Mitton was in the West Riding of Yorkshire. Little Mitton Hall, now a pub, restaurant and hotel complex, was built in the Tudor period and enlarged in the 19th century. It has a superb 16th-century, galleried Great Hall.

(D) Occupying a commanding position above the Ribble, Mitton church mostly dates from the late 13th century, although the west tower was built later in 1438. It is chiefly renowned for the Shireburn Chapel, added by Sir Richard Shireburn, the builder of Stonyhurst, in 1594 and containing his tomb and those of many of his successors. Next to the church stands Great Mitton Hall, which has an impressive 17th century gable end overlooking the river.

(E) Low Moor is an interesting example of a planned, 19th-century industrial community, built on the grid pattern to house the workers at the adjacent cotton mill. The mill, founded in 1782 and enlarged after 1799, was an enormous building. It was finally demolished in 1967 and its riverside site is now occupied by modern houses. Low Moor church, a fine example of Victorian Gothic, dates from 1867-69.

14. Downham and Sawley Abbey

Start/Parking: Downham – grid reference 785441.

Distance: 6½ miles (10.5km) for the full walk; there is a shorter version of 5½ miles (8.9km).

Category: Moderate.

Refreshments: Assheton Arms at Downham, tea room attached to Downham post office, Spread Eagle at Sawley.

Terrain: Mostly on tracks and field paths, some of which are likely to be muddy, with a few short and modest climbs; some of the stiles are in poor condition.

OS Maps: Landranger 103, Outdoor Leisure 41.

Public transport: Buses from Clitheroe.

What you'll discover

The village of Downham, a prime candidate for the title of prettiest village in Lancashire, nestles below Pendle Hill and the distinctive bulk of the hill broods over the landscape for much of the walk. There are also impressive and extensive views across the Ribble valley on the first half of the route as you descend to the banks of the Ribble by the meagre but attractively sited ruins of Sawley Abbey.

Route Directions

Start by turning left out of the car park, cross the bridge over Downham Beck and turn left to walk up through the village towards the church **(A)** at the top end. Just before reaching the church, turn right along a lane and at a wall corner turn left onto a path. Pass in front of a house to go through a gate, keep ahead through another and head gently uphill along the left edge of a field, bearing right to climb a stone stile.

As you continue over the brow of the hill, a superb view unfolds ahead over the Ribble valley. Descend to climb a stone stile onto a lane just to the right of the field corner, go through a gate opposite, walk across a field and go through a gate to the left of a farm. Keep ahead to go through another one and continue along a track which descends to pass under a railway bridge and go through a gate. Keep ahead to go through another gate to the right of a barn, walk across the next field and on the far side, turn right to continue along the field edge above Swanside Beck.

Climb a stile, descend to cross a footbridge over a tributary stream and continue across the next field, making for a stone stile in the left-hand corner. After climbing it, cross the old packhorse bridge over Swanside Beck, climb a stile, bear left and head steeply uphill to climb another stile at the top. Head diagonally across a field, climb a stile near the corner and walk along the right edge of the next field. Climb a stile, keep ahead to go through a gate, continue in the same direction across the middle of the next field and climb a stile on the far side. Keep ahead along a farm track for a few metres and climb another stile onto the busy A59.

Cross carefully, climb a stile on the opposite side and head downhill across a field to a ladder stile. Climb it, continue downhill along an enclosed, tree-lined path, ford a stream and keep ahead to climb a stile. Cross a tarmac track, climb a stile opposite and walk across a field, making for a stone stile just to the left of a gate. Climb that and bear slightly left across the next field, descending gently to a stile. To the left, there is a fine view of the ruins of Sawley Abbey. After climbing the stile, walk through the car park of the Spread Eagle Hotel to emerge onto a road. The entrance to the abbey **(B)** is to the left.

Turn right along a lane beside the River Ribble and follow it as it bends right and heads uphill to the A59. Again cross with care, turn left and at a public footpath sign, turn right through a gate and walk along the right edge of a field. Continue along a hedge-lined track, go through a gate and follow the track to the right towards a farm. Before entering the farmyard, turn left off the track and walk along the right edge of a field to a stile. Climb it, keep ahead to join a track, pass to the left of a barn and go through two gates in quick succession.

Bear right across a field corner and keep along the right edge of

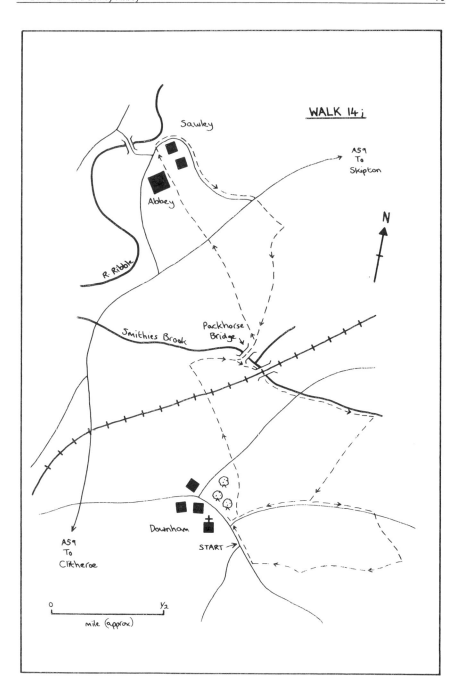

WALK 14j

Sawley

A59
To
Skipton

N

Abbey

R. Ribble

Smithies Brook

Packhorse
Bridge

Downham

A59
To
Clitheroe

START →

0   ½
mile (approx)

the field to a gate. Go through and continue along the right edge of the next field, descending gently to go through another gate. Descend steeply to re-cross the old packhorse bridge – briefly joining the outward route – but instead of turning right, keep ahead along the left edge of a field, by woodland on the left. Turn left between gateposts to continue along the right edge of the wood, pass under a railway bridge just to the right of a viaduct, go through a gate and keep ahead along the left edge of two fields to eventually emerge, via a gate, onto a lane.

Take the track opposite, passing to the right of a former mill beyond which you climb a stone stile. Continue along a track, go through a gate and keep ahead alongside a beck to a footbridge. Do not cross it but turn sharp right and head uphill to climb a stone stile in the top corner of the field. Walk across a field corner to climb another stile, continue in the same direction to climb another one and head uphill across the next field. Climb a stile at the top edge, keep along the left edge of a field and climb a stile onto a lane.

Turn right and follow the lane back to Downham if doing the shorter walk. For the full walk, turn left and after a quarter of a mile, turn right through a gate, at a public footpath sign, and walk along the right edge of a field to another gate. Go through, bear left along the top left edge of the next field, passing to the right of a farm, and go through a gate in the field corner. Keep ahead to climb a stone stile just to the left of a hedge corner and walk along the right edge of a field. After about 50 metres, turn right through a gate, keep along the right edge of a field and where the field edge bears right, keep straight ahead to first ford a brook and climb a stile on the far side.

Bear slightly right across the next field, climb a stone stile in the far right corner and head across a field corner to climb another stone stile. Continue across the next field corner and ford a beck to the right of a stile. Turn right and head across a field towards the cottages of Downham, rejoining the beck by a waymarked post and keeping by it to climb a stone stile on the edge of the village. Continue along a tarmac track in front of cottages, turn right at a T-junction and turn left by the bridge to return to the start.

Features of Interest

(A) Downham is remarkably attractive and unspoilt. From the church, hall and pub at the top end of the village, old cottages descend to the beck, bridge and green at the bottom end and there are no modern intrusions to mar this idyllic scene. The church occupies a fine position overlooking the village and Pendle Hill. Apart from the medieval tower, it was mainly rebuilt in 1909-10. Inside are memorials to the Assheton family, occupants of the adjacent Downham Hall.

(B) The small and relatively poor Cistercian abbey of Sawley or Salley was founded in 1148. It was dissolved on the orders of Henry VIII in 1536 but temporarily re-occupied by monks during the rebellion of the Pilgrimage of Grace. After the suppression of that rebellion, the last abbot of Sawley was executed, suffering the same fate as that of his close neighbour at Whalley.

The ruins of Sawley Abbey

```
┌─────────────────────────────────────────────────┐
│ ┌─────────────────────────────────────────────┐ │
│ ║                                             ║ │
│ ║            15. Pendle Hill                  ║ │
│ ║                                             ║ │
│ └─────────────────────────────────────────────┘ │
└─────────────────────────────────────────────────┘
```

Start/Parking: Barley, car park and picnic site—grid reference 823403.

Distance: 6 miles (9.7km).

Category: Fairly strenuous.

Refreshments: Pendle Inn, Barley Mow and tea room at Barley.

Terrain: Although most of the paths are good, much of the route is across open moorland, with some steep climbs and descents, and should not be attempted in bad weather, especially in wintry or misty conditions.

OS Maps: Landranger 103, Outdoor Leisure 41.

Public transport: Infrequent buses from Clitheroe and Burnley, also a Pendle Witch Hopper 'Leisure Links' service operates on Sundays and Bank Holidays from May to September.

What you'll discover

On many of the routes in this book, the unmistakable profile of Pendle Hill can be seen brooding over the landscape and acting as a magnet to walkers. For those familiar with it, Pendle is a hill of many moods; welcoming and benign in fine weather but forbidding and mysterious in gloomy conditions, as befits a hill closely identified with 17th-century witchcraft. The walk begins by visiting two of the villages at its foot and then climbs, via the well-waymarked Pendle Way, to the 1831ft (555m) summit. From here, there are the most superb and extensive views over the Ribble valley.

Route Directions

The presence of Pendle Hill **(A)** is felt throughout the walk, starting with the view of it from the car park. Begin by turning right out of the car park, take the first turning on the left, sign-posted to Burnley, and head uphill. Where the road curves right, turn left, at a public footpath sign to Newchurch, along a track (Bridge End). After passing in front of a row of cottages, the enclosed track continues uphill and at the top look out for a stile on the right.

Climb it, head uphill along the right edge of a field, climb a stile to the right of a farmhouse and turn right along a track to a road. Turn left downhill into Newchurch in Pendle **(B)** and at a public footpath sign, turn right and ascend steps to the left of a toilet block, here joining the Pendle Way. Climb a stile at the top of the steps, keep ahead and turn left over another stile. Head uphill across a field, making for a waymarked post just to the left of a ladder stile, and turn left alongside a wall, still uphill, to a stile in the top corner.

Climb it, continue along the right edge of the next field, crossing a broken down wall, and at the corner of a conifer plantation, turn right over a stile. Head downhill along the right edge of the plantation, turn left over a stile and follow a path through the conifers, later descending steps to emerge from them. The path bends right downhill to cross a footbridge over a stream and then curves right to a Pendle Way footpath post. Turn left, climb steps. cross another footbridge and go through a gate onto a track by the end of Lower Ogden reservoir.

Turn left uphill, later keeping along the left edge of conifers, and at a fork take the left-hand track. Climb a stone stile in front of the dam of Upper Ogden reservoir, head uphill alongside the dam and keep ahead above the reservoir. Climb another stile, continue along the side of Ogden Clough and after climbing a ladder stile, the path heads uphill. About 100 metres after fording a stream, turn right, at a Pendle Way sign, and head steeply uphill above Boar Clough. The well-waymarked route – plenty of cairns and Pendle Way signs to show the way – winds steadily uphill across the open moorland, fording several streams, to eventually reach the trig point **(C)** at the 1831ft (555m) summit.

Continue past the trig point to a wall, briefly bear right alongside it and then turn sharp right to descend steeply, via a well-constructed path, to a kissing gate. Go through, turn right and follow a series of yellow-topped posts across a field, keeping to the right of a farm, to a stile. Climb it, turn left downhill, bearing slightly right to descend into a gully, and head up again. Turn right over a stile, keep along a path to a farm, pass to the left of the farm buildings and go through a kissing gate.

Walk along a partly tree-lined path, by a stream on the right, climb a stile and continue along a fence-lined path, now with the stream on the left. Recross it, head down to go through a kissing gate and turn left along a tarmac track. Continue to a footbridge, turn right over it and turn left alongside the stream, on the left again. Cross another footbridge, climb a stile and continue alongside the stream to a stone stile.

Climb it, turn right along a road through Barley and at a Pendle Way sign, continue along a path that runs parallel to the road along the edge of a children's play area. Turn left over a footbridge and follow a path back to the car park.

Features of Interest

(A) It was in the early 17th century that Pendle Hill and the surrounding area became associated with stories of witchcraft but the trial and execution of the Pendle witches has to be seen against the background of general superstition at the time. After the accession of James I to the English throne in 1603, something of an anti-witch hysteria developed as, while king of Scotland, James had developed an obsession with witchcraft and had written a book on the subject.

The trouble in the Pendle area seems to have originated from a feud between two local families, both headed by two old women nicknamed Chattox and Demdike. They and various members of their families were alleged to have practised witchcraft and, after local enquiries, were sent for trial at Lancaster Castle. The verdict was a foregone conclusion; all nine of the accused were found guilty and hanged on 20 August 1612.

Details of this event were written down at the time and subsequently publicised by Thomas Potts, clerk to the judge. Later books on the subject, notably Harrison Ainsworth's The Lancashire Witches and Robert Neill's Mist Over Pendle, further popularised the episode and have helped to turn it, and the area that the witches came from, into a tourist attraction.

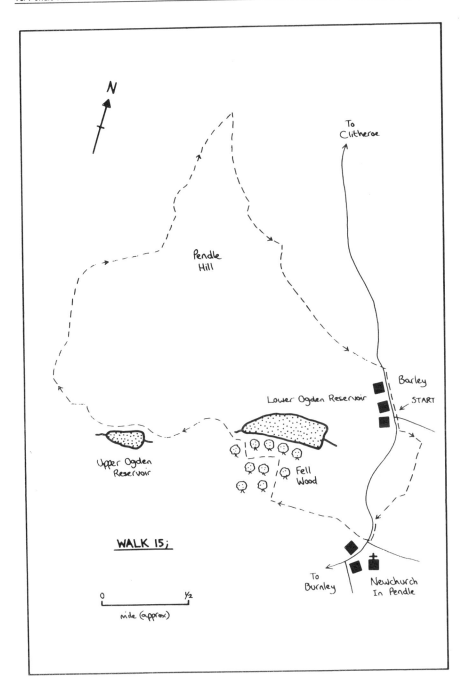

N

To
Clitheroe

Pendle
Hill

Barley

START

Lower Ogden Reservoir

Upper Ogden
Reservoir

Fell
Wood

WALK 15;

0   ½

mile (approx)

To
Burnley

Newchurch
In Pendle

(B) Two particularly ugly model witches sit outside the Witches Galore shop in the village of Newchurch in Pendle. Inside the shop is full of books, souvenirs and general information about the Pendle witches. The church, new in 1544, was largely rebuilt in the 18th century. It is notable for the gap in the stonework near the base of the tower, called the 'eye of God', which is believed to watch over the local people and protect them from evil.

(C) From the trig point on the Beacon or Big End of Pendle, the panoramic views are magnificent, especially looking across the Ribble valley to the Bowland Fells and Yorkshire Dales.

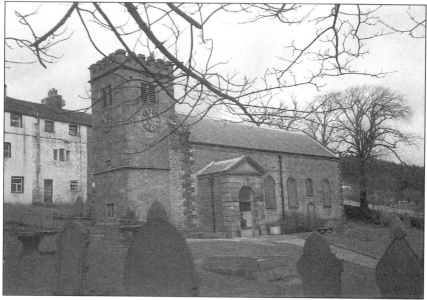

The 'Eye of God' at Newchurch-in-Pendle

16. Wycoller

Start/Parking: Wycoller Country Park, Haworth Road car park – grid reference 937394.

Distance: 2½ miles (4km).

Category: Easy.

Refreshments: Café at Wycoller Craft Centre.

Terrain: Clear and well-waymarked paths and tracks all the way with two short and easy climbs.

OS Maps: Landranger 103, Outdoor Leisure 21.

Public transport: None.

What you'll discover

The focal point of this short but highly attractive walk is the secluded and fascinating former handloom weaving village of Wycoller, complete with old cottages, ruined hall and a collection of interesting and varied bridges over the beck. The first half of the route is along the side of the valley, with outstanding views of Pendle Hill and the edge of the Brontë moors; the second half mostly keeps beside Wycoller Beck into the village.

Route Directions

From the car park comes the first of a series of superb views over the Wycoller valley, with the village immediately below, the towers of the town hall and church at Colne in the distance, and Pendle Hill on the horizon. Descend steps from the car park to follow a downhill path, bearing right to a kissing gate. Go through, continue downhill and where a path crosses, turn left over a stile.

Walk across a field, climb a stile, head steadily uphill by a wire fence on the right and go through a wall gap. Continue through another wall gap and at a fork, take the left-hand uphill path. Go through a wall gap, by a waymarked post, and continue uphill in the same direction to a wall corner where you bear right to a ladder stile. Climb it and keep by the wall on your right to join a tarmac drive.

The drive heads downhill below the rocks of Foster's Leap **(A)**, going round sharp right and left bends and passing to the right of a bungalow. Keep ahead to go through a gate to the right of Foster's Leap Farm, bear left at a wall corner, climb a ladder stile and follow a series of footpath posts across a field towards farm buildings. Descend to go through a kissing gate, cross a footbridge over Wycoller Beck and in front of a barn, turn right onto a track.

Walk along this beautiful, tree-lined track – the beck is sometimes on the right and sometimes on the left – to a T-junction. Turn right to cross a bridge and continue along the track, with the beck on the left, into Wycoller, passing the Clam Bridge **(B)**.

In the village climb steps beside the ruined hall and follow a path steadily uphill, by the upright stone slabs of one of the Vaccary Walls **(C)** on the left. The path, part of the old coach road to Wycoller Hall, leads back to the start.

Wycoller Hall

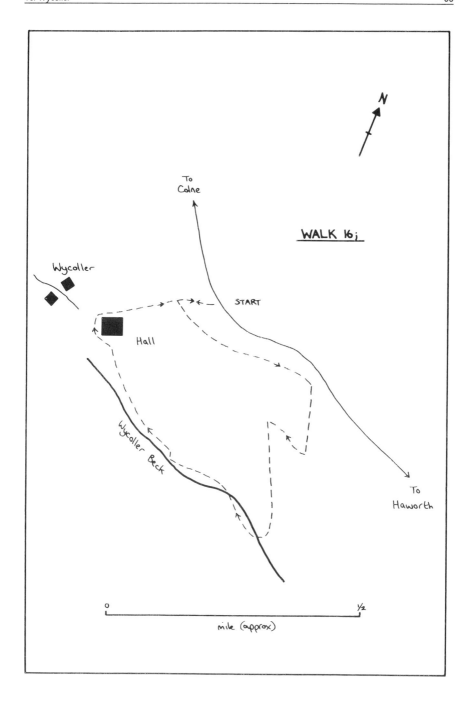

Features of Interest

(A) These rocks are named after Foster Cunliffe, a relative of the Cunliffe family who lived at Wycoller Hall. He is supposed to have jumped from boulder to boulder but whether he carried out this daring feat for a bet or just bravado is not known.

(B) In the 17th century Wycoller, formerly a secluded farming hamlet in the ancient forest of Trawden, developed into a handloom weaving centre. When handloom weaving was at its height in the early 19th century, the population rose to around 350 but the subsequent introduction of the power loom and the village's remoteness led to a steady decline and it eventually became virtually abandoned and derelict. The process of revival began in 1973 when Lancashire County Council purchased the estate. The village was designated a conservation area and the area around it was made into a country park. As a result, this idyllic and historic hamlet and its surrounding landscape have become a tourist venue, especially popular with walkers.

Two of the main attractions are the bridges and the ruined hall. Seven bridges cross the beck near Wycoller and three of these are particularly interesting. The Clam Bridge, passed about a quarter of a mile before reaching the village, comprises a single grit-stone slab thought to be over 1000 years old. In the village itself near the hall are the Clapper Bridge, a simple construction of stone slabs supported by piers, probably dating from around the end of the 18th century, and the picturesque medieval Pack-horse Bridge.

Wycoller Hall was built in the 16th century and enlarged in the late 18th century by its last owner, Henry Owen Cunliffe. This was when the fireplace, its most impressive feature, was constructed. After he died in 1818 leaving substantial debts, the hall was left unoccupied, fell into ruin was used as a source of building stone. It has strong associations with the Brontës, who lived not far away at Haworth. Charlotte Brontë is thought to have been a frequent visitor and some believe that Ferndean Manor in *Jane Eyre* is based on it. The 17th-century aisled barn next to the hall has been restored as an Information Centre.

(C) One of the most distinctive and unusual features of the landscape around Wycoller are these walls of upright stone slabs, some of which will have been noticed earlier on the walk. They are called Vaccary Walls – vaccaries were medieval cattle farms – and were built to mark the farm boundaries and to enclose the cattle. Most of them are believed to date from the 12th to 15th centuries.

17. Hurstwood, Worsthorne and Gorple Road

Start/Parking: Hurstwood, car park and picnic site — grid reference 882314.

Distance: 6 miles (9.7km).

Category: Moderate.

Refreshments: Bay Horse and Crooked Billet pubs at Worsthorne.

Terrain: Easy at the beginning and end but the middle part of the route involves rough moorland walking on indistinct paths.

OS Maps: Landranger 103, Outdoor Leisure 21.

Public transport: Occasional buses from Burnley and Nelson.

What you'll discover

Most of this exhilarating walk is across the austere, open Pennine moorland that lies to the east of Burnley. There are fine and extensive views in all directions and reservoirs and conifer plantations break up the bare landscape in places. The route includes two attractive villages and part of it follows an ancient trans-Pennine routeway.

Route Directions

Leave the car park, walk across the picnic area and at a T-junction, turn left through a gate to follow a tarmac drive to Cant Clough reservoir. Go through a gate to the left of the dam and turn left along an uphill track, which curves left to a waymarked footpath post.

Turn sharp right (almost doubling back) along a track which bends right above the reservoir to reach a T-junction. Turn left and follow a faint but discernible path across the open moorland, head-

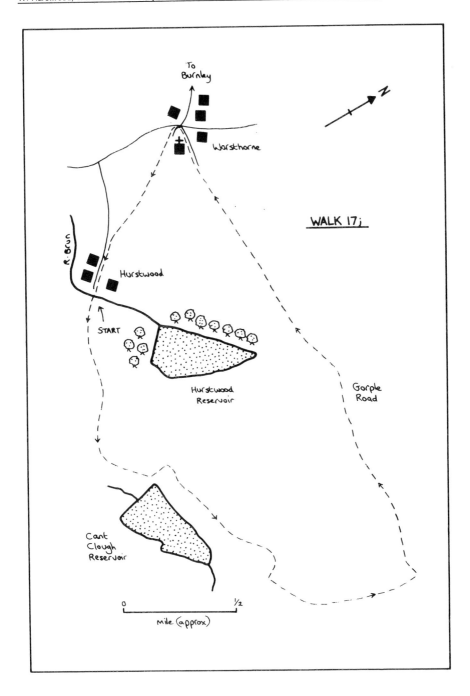

To
Burnley

Worsthorne

WALK 17;

R. Brun

Hurstwood

START

Hurstwood
Reservoir

Gorple
Road

Cant
Clough
Reservoir

0   ½
mile (approx)

Spenser's Cottage

ing in the direction of the prominent group of rocks – the Hare Stones – on the horizon. On joining a clearer path, follow it steadily uphill along the left rim of Rams Clough. This is a permissive path, marked by a series of posts, which eventually reaches a broad track just to the left of a bridge.

Turn left along it – this is Gorple Road **(A)** – to continue across the moorland. Ahead are views over Burnley down in the valley, with Pendle Hill on the skyline. After going through a gate, the track becomes enclosed by walls and continues more or less in a straight line – later becoming a tarmac lane – gently downhill into the village of Worsthorne **(B)**.

At a T-junction turn left , keep along the left edge of a triangular green and in front of the Bay Horse Inn, turn left again to pass to the right of the church. Turn right along Green Terrace and where the road ends, keep ahead along an enclosed, paved path to a kissing gate. Go through, walk across a field – still on a partly paved path – climb a stone stile and continue along the left edge of the next field to another stone stile. Climb that, keep ahead first along an enclosed track, then continue along the left edge of the next field and climb a stone stile onto a lane.

Turn left into Hurstwood **(C)**, bear left and then right to cross a bridge over the River Brun and keep ahead to return to the start.

Features of Interest

(A) This is an old pack-horse trail across the Pennines between Worsthorne and Heptonstall, a particularly fine example of many such trans-Pennine routeways along which commodities such as lime, coal and cloth would have been carried.

(B) Worsthorne has grown in recent years but still has a number of attractive old cottages, dating from the 17th to the 19th centuries, in the village centre near the green. Overlooking the green is the handsome Victorian church.

(C) Little more than a hamlet, Hurstwood has some delightful old cottages and is attractively situated on the little River Brun, by woodland and on the edge of the moors. Its most prominent building, Hurstwood Hall, dates from 1579 and almost opposite, and of similar age, is Spenser's House, thought to be the cottage in which the Elizabethan poet Edmund Spenser lived for a while. He wrote 'The Faerie Queen' and was a contemporary of William Shakespeare.

18. Witton Country Park and Hoghton Tower

Start/Parking: Witton Country Park, Billinge Wood, Killiard Lane car park – grid reference 654282.

Distance: The full walk is 9 miles (14.5km), the shorter version which omits the loop around Hoghton is 5½ miles (8.9km).

Category: Fairly strenuous.

Refreshments: Butler's Arms at Pleasington, Royal Oak at Riley Green, tea-room at Hoghton Tower.

Terrain: Undulating route, across fields, along riverside meadows and through woodland, mostly on well-defined tracks and footpaths some of which are likely to be muddy at times, a few steep though short ascents and descents.

OS Maps: Landranger 103, Explorer 19.

Public transport: An occasional circular bus service between Blackburn and Pleasington, also buses from Blackburn pass within 1 mile of the start at the junction of Preston New Road and Billinge End Road.

What you'll discover

There is a choice between walking the complete route or doing a shorter version. From the wooded heights of Billinge Hill, you descend through Witton Country Park into the valley of the River Darwen. Much of the remainder of the route is either beside or above the river, until the final stretch where you climb out of the valley and follow a splendid ridge path across the Yellow Hills, so called from their profusion of gorse bushes. There is much pleasant riverside and woodland walking and some extensive views from the higher points. The most dramatic part of the route comes on the full walk, which does an additional loop around the base of the abrupt hill crowned by Hoghton Tower – well worth a visit – and through the thickly-wooded Hoghton Gorge.

Hoghton Gorge

Route Directions

Climb a stile in the corner of the car park **(A)**, turn left and head downhill alongside a wall bordering Billinge Wood. The path bends right away from the wall and continues down to a tarmac drive. Turn sharp left along it and after going through a kissing gate beside a cattle-grid, turn right down to another kissing gate.

Go through that and head downhill through a narrow strip of woodland, climbing two pairs of stiles, to reach a junction of paths. Turn right down steps, cross a footbridge over a stream, bear left and continue initially above the stream, later descending steps to join the stream. Cross another footbridge over it and keep ahead along the right edge of a meadow to reach a bridge over the River Darwen.

Do not cross it but turn right alongside the river, later bearing right away from it across a meadow to climb a stile. Climb steps and continue across a playing field, rejoining the river and keeping by it to reach a road by two adjacent bridges. Again do not cross either but bear right across another playing field, in the direction of the church seen ahead, to reach a track on the far side. Cross the track and keep in the same direction, taking the left-hand one of two paths ahead, through a shallow gully and on along a track to emerge onto a road opposite the Butler's Arms. To the right is Pleasington Priory **(B)**.

Walk along the road opposite through a new housing area, then along a track and bear right to climb a stile. Continue along a path, climb a stile, keep ahead and descend to another stile. Climb that and another one, keep by a wall on the right, climb yet another stile and continue along a track which bears right down to a bridge over the River Darwen. In front of the bridge, turn right over a stile, keep beside the river, climb another stile and follow it around a left bend up to a junction of paths.

At this point, turn right if you are doing the shorter walk, which omits the loop around Hoghton Tower and through Hoghton Gorge.

For those wishing to do the full walk, turn left over a bridge, turn right around the end of cottages and walk along a lane through the hamlet of Hoghton Bottoms. At a junction, turn left along Viaduct Road and opposite a farm, turn right over a stile and keep ahead to climb another one. Head uphill, alongside a wall bordering a conifer plantation, and the path bears slightly left away from it up to a stile. Climb that, keep ahead to cross the railway line – take care here as the trains are fairly frequent – continue uphill through woodland and bear right alongside a wall. Keeping by the wall, climb a succession of stiles and finally walk along a track to reach the tarmac drive of Hoghton Tower **(C)**.

Turn left if the house is open and you wish to visit it; otherwise keep ahead to go through a kissing gate and head gently uphill along the left edge of a field to a ladder stile. Continue along an enclosed track, climb a ladder stile and keep straight ahead across a field to climb another ladder stile on the far side. To the left is a fine view of Hoghton Tower. Continue across the next field, heading gently downhill to climb a ladder stile in the bottom left-hand corner, and walk along a track to reach the main road beside the Royal Oak at Riley Green.

Turn left and at a public footpath sign, turn left along a track. At a bend, keep ahead through a kissing gate, follow a track steeply downhill, climb a stile and the track swings left down to the banks of the Darwen. Climb a ladder stile and continue along a riverside path

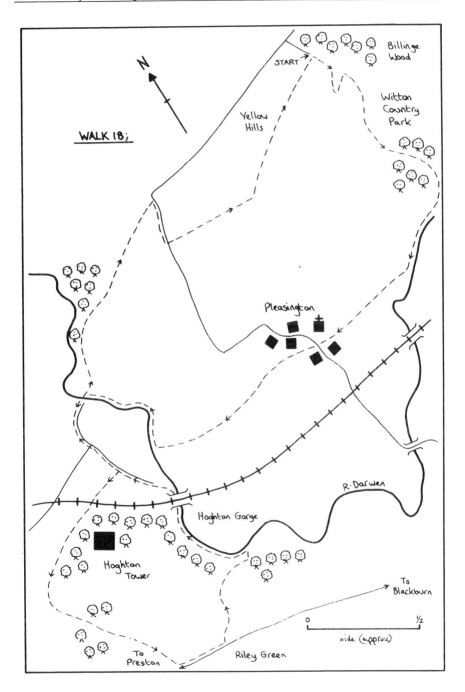

N

WALK 18;

START

Billinge Wood

Witton Country Park

Yellow Hills

Pleasington

R. Darwen

Hoghton Gorge

Hoghton Tower

To Blackburn

0   ½

mile (approx)

To Preston

Riley Green

through the wooded and dramatic Hoghton Gorge, passing by a weir and going under a railway viaduct **(D)**.

The path widens into a track and then becomes a lane. Keep along it, rejoining the outward route, and retrace your steps through Hoghton Bottoms to the bridge over the Darwen.

After crossing the bridge, you pick up the shorter version of the walk at a public footpath sign.

Climb the stile in front, keep ahead in front of farm buildings, turn left in front of a fence and climb another stile. Walk along a track to rejoin the river, later climbing above it along the right edge of steeply sloping woodland. Below the river can be seen flowing through another wooded gorge. At the point where the track enters woodland and about 50 metres before it curves left, bear right and head steeply uphill, by the right edge of trees and gorse bushes. Continue along a grassy ledge, still by the right edge of woodland, bear left through a gap in the trees to ford a small stream and head steeply uphill again, now with woodland on the right, to a stile at a wall corner. Climb it and continue uphill across a field towards a farm, joining and keeping alongside a hedge on the left. Go through a gap, keep ahead to climb a stile in front of the farm buildings and continue along a track, passing to the left of the farm.

Go through a gate and follow the track – now a tarmac one – to reach a road at a bend. Turn right, at a public footpath sign turn left along the track to Maiden House Farm and on along the left edge of a field to a stile. Climb it, keep ahead, parallel to the left edge of a field, climb another stile just in front of a gate and continue by a partial line of trees on the left to a stile on the edge of woodland. Climb it and the path bends left and heads uphill through the trees to a track. Turn left, continue uphill towards houses and look out for a turn to the right onto a path which heads gently uphill to a stile.

Climb it, keep along the right edge of a field above a disused quarry and climb another stile. The final part of the walk is a grand ridge path, with extensive views on both sides, which you follow in a straight line across the Yellow Hills, climbing two more stiles to return to the start.

Features of Interest

(A) Witton Country Park, around 480 acres of wooded hillside, parkland and grassland on the western edge of Blackburn, occupies part of the former estates of the Feilden family. Some of the ornamental gardens remain and the stable block, the only part of the hall to survive, houses a Visitor Centre and displays of old farm tools, carriages and machinery. On the northern edge of the park, the thickly wooded Billinge Hill rises to over 800ft.

(B) The Roman Catholic Pleasington Priory, built in 1819, is an early example of the Gothic Revival.

(C) Although built in the Elizabethan period, the battlemented gatehouse and hilltop location – 650ft (197m) above sea level – give Hoghton Tower a medieval, fortress-like appearance. In the 18th century the family abandoned the house and it became semi-derelict but the return of Sir Henry de Hoghton after 1870 inaugurated a period of restoration. In the superb Banqueting Hall is the table at which, it is alleged, James I knighted a loin of beef – hence sirloin – because he was so pleased with the hospitality he received while on a visit to Hoghton Tower in 1617.

(D) The impressive Victorian railway viaduct carries the East Lancashire line, between Preston and Blackburn, over the Hoghton Gorge.

19. Roddlesworth Woodland and Darwen Tower

Start/Parking: Roddlesworth Information Centre, next to the Royal Arms to the south of Tockholes – grid reference 665215.

Distance: 6½ miles (10.5km).

Category: Moderate.

Refreshments: Royal Arms at start.

Terrain: Generally well-defined woodland paths and moorland tracks, some modest climbs.

OS Maps: Landrangers 103 and 109, Explorer 19.

Public transport: Infrequent bus service from Blackburn.

What you'll discover

The walk falls into two distinctive and clearly defined halves. The first part is through the beautiful woodland that clothes the sides of the Roddlesworth valley. In complete contrast the second half takes you across open moorland to Darwen Tower, both a grand viewpoint and a prominent landmark over much of the surrounding area. In the past there were several small coal mines on Darwen Moor and many of the tracks were created by the miners.

Route Directions

Go through a kissing gate in front of the Royal Arms and head downhill into woodland. Bear right, cross a track and keep ahead towards Upper Roddlesworth reservoir. Turn left alongside a fence above the reservoir, cross a brook and continue through the wooded Roddlesworth valley, with the river on the right **(A)**.

Cross a footbridge over the river and continue along the right

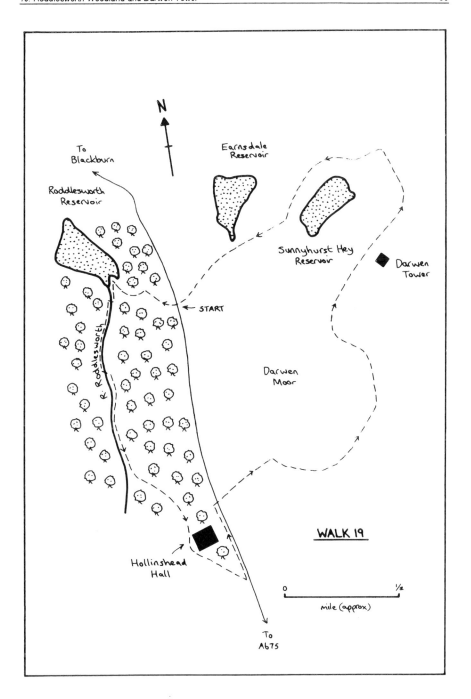

WALK 19

bank, first ascending and later descending steps, to reach Halliwell Fold Bridge. Turn left to re-cross the river and at a footpath sign to Hollinshead Hall, turn right along the left bank again. The track climbs gently and bears away from the river. Go through a gate, descend to the scanty ruins of Hollinshead Hall **(B)** and continue past them, emerging from the woodland to reach a lane.

Turn left, at a public footpath sign to Lyons Den turn right over a stile and follow a winding, grassy track steadily uphill across Darwen Moor, heading towards a ridge. At a fork just below the ridge, continue uphill along the left-hand track to a waymarked post and keep ahead to go through a kissing gate. The track curves gradually left towards Darwen Tower. Go through another kissing gate and at a fork immediately ahead, take the left-hand track. At a marker stone with a tower carved on it, bear left off the main track to continue winding across the moor, following a series of similar marker stones. A brief detour to the right brings you to the tower **(C)**.

Return to the track, turn right and at a fork, head downhill along the left-hand track. Shortly after going through a gate, turn left along an enclosed path, climb a stone stile and continue to a concrete track. Bear right, pass beside a gate, continue down to a T-junction and turn left. At a fork beside a house, take the left-hand upper track, which keeps above Earnsdale reservoir on the right and below Sunnyhurst Hey reservoir on the left, and look out for another fork by a short stretch of walling on both sides of the track.

Take the right-hand, grassy track which descends to a revolving metal gate. Go through, continue gently downhill, go through a kissing gate and head uphill, by a fence on the left, to a stile. Climb it, keep ahead to go through a gate in the field corner and turn left along a tree-lined track which emerges onto the road by the Royal Arms.

Features of Interest

(A) Liverpool Corporation was responsible for both the reservoirs and the woods around them, one of the largest areas of mainly broad-leaved woodland in Lancashire. The Roddlesworth reservoirs were constructed in the middle of the 19th century. Later on the surrounding land was acquired and the woods were planted from 1904 onwards to prevent erosion of the valley sides.

(B) Although there is evidence of earlier houses on the site, the remains mainly comprise the foundations of an 18th-century hall, once the manor house for Tockholes. The impressive Well House nearby is the only surviving building.

(C) Darwen Tower, built in 1897 to commemorate Queen Victoria's Diamond Jubilee, is a familiar local landmark. It is 86ft (26m) high and stands at a height of 1225ft (371m). The extensive views range from the mills and terraces of Blackburn and Darwen, dominated by the Venetian-style chimney of India Mill, across to the West Pennine Moors, Bowland Fells and the Fylde, including, in clear conditions, Blackpool Tower.

The wooded valley of the River Roddlesworth

20. Haslingden Grane

Start/Parking: Clough Head picnic site – grid reference 754233.

Distance: 3½ miles (5.6km).

Category: Moderate.

Refreshments: There is often a kiosk in the car park.

Terrain: Well-waymarked but expect some rough moorland walking and muddy, badly-drained paths in places.

OS Maps: Landranger 103. Explorer 19.

Public transport: Buses from Blackburn and Haslingden.

What you'll discover

Haslingden Grane is situated in the old Forest of Rossendale, an area of open moorland and wooded cloughs formerly used for hunting. Even today, despite the proximity of industry, large towns and busy motorways, the forest still manages to retain something of its previous isolation and wildness. The disused quarry at the start and the ruins of farms and handloom weavers' cottages, conifer plantations and reservoirs passed on the walk, illustrate the many and varied uses to which the Grane valley has been put throughout the centuries.

Route Directions

Begin by going through a gate in the car park **(A)** and taking the path sign-posted 'Calf Hey Trail'. Go through another gate onto the road, turn left and at a sign 'Path to Calf Hey', turn right through a gate and follow a winding, downhill path, passing through another gate onto a tarmac drive.

Turn right over a stile and head uphill along a walled track above Calf Hey Reservoir. The track goes through two gates and over a stile

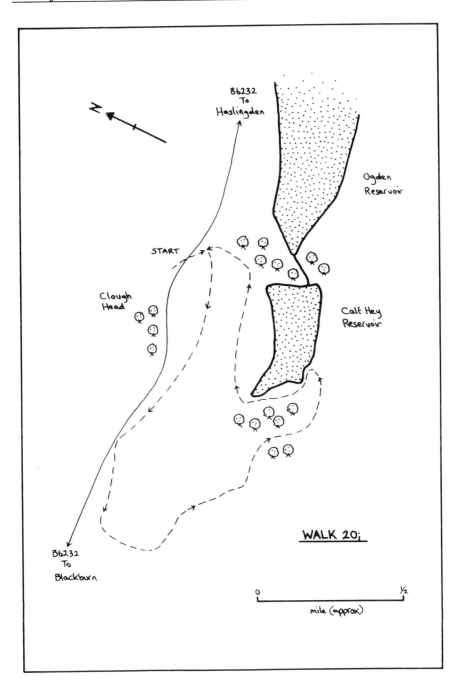

to emerge onto the road again via a ladder stile. Turn left and at a Rossendale Way sign, turn left over a stile, walk along a track, turn right at the next footpath sign and the track now curves left around the head of the Grane valley. Turn right to cross a stream in front of a broken wall and after about 50 metres, turn left through a wall gap and walk along a moorland path, passing by several ruined farms. The route is well-waymarked and after the second farm you join a walled track and follow it down to the ruins of the next farm.

Turn first left and then right alongside a fence on the left, cross a stream and after climbing a stile, keep along the right edge of conifer woodland, heading down into a wooded clough. Turn left at a Rossendale Way sign down to a T-junction, turn right and continue downhill, turning sharp left to cross a footbridge over a stream. Keep ahead through trees and at the next stream, turn left alongside it to a track.

Turn left and follow the track as it bears right around the end of Calf Hey Reservoir **(B)**, crossing two streams. After going through a gate, the track – now a tarmac one – curves right to continue above

Handloom weavers' cottages, Haslingden Grane

the reservoir, passing the ruins of Ormerods and Hartley House **(C)**. It later curves left and passes through a kissing gate into Calf Hey car park.

At a footpath sign to Clough Head, turn left through a gate, ascend steps and continue along a path to emerge onto a tarmac drive at a bend. From here take the path ahead, picking up the outward route, and retrace your steps to the start.

Features of Interest

(A) The car park and pleasant picnic area at Clough Head occupies the site of a quarry opened in the 1890s. Once, there were many quarries in the area, as Rossendale flagstone was widely used to pave the towns and cities of Victorian England, including the streets of London.

(B) Calf Hey is one of three adjacent reservoirs constructed in the Grane valley to provide water for the nearby towns.

(C) The ruined cottages at Ormerods and Hartley House were used for handloom weaving in the early years of the Industrial Revolution, before the advent of power looms drove the industry into factories and put many handloom weavers out of work.

21. Mere Sands Wood and Rufford Old Hall

Start/Parking: Rufford, Station car park – grid reference 467156.

Distance: 6 miles (9.7km).

Category: Easy.

Refreshments: Hesketh Arms at Rufford, Rufford Arms Hotel just before reaching the canal towards the end of the walk, tea room at Rufford Old Hall.

Terrain: Flat walking on clear paths, tracks and canal towpaths.

OS Maps: Landranger 108, Pathfinder 699.

Public transport: Buses from Southport, Chorley, Preston and Ormskirk; trains from Preston and Ormskirk.

What you'll discover

A large proportion of this walk in the flat countryside of the West Lancashire coastal plain is beside water: either by the River Douglas, Leeds-Liverpool Canal or drainage channels. Such flat terrain gives a series of extensive and unimpeded views, looking towards the coast and across to the westernmost edge of the Pennines, and there are several fine wooded stretches. The National Trust property of Rufford Old Hall is well worth a visit and there is also the opportunity to explore a most attractive nature reserve.

Route Directions

Turn right out of the car park and just before the bridge over the River Douglas, turn right through a gate and walk along the top of an embankment above the river. After climbing a stile the river curves left but the path continues ahead along the embankment, now above Eller Brook, to reach a lane by Wham Bridge.

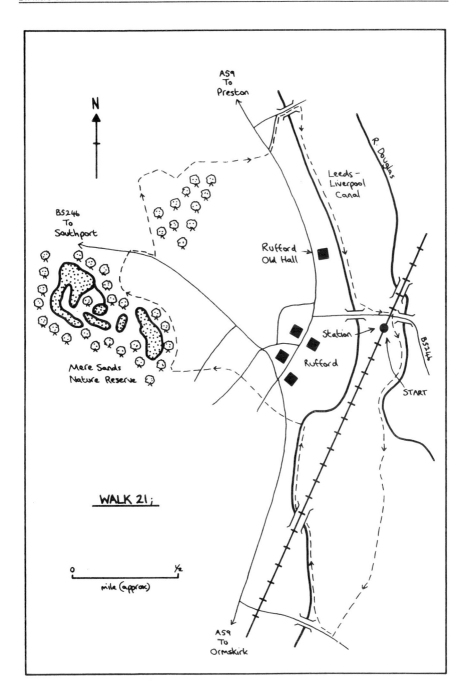

WALK 21;

0 _____ ½

mile (approx)

Rufford Old Hall

Turn right and on the approach to the next bridge, turn left beside a barrier down to the canal, turn sharp right to pass under the bridge and continue along the towpath of the Leeds-Liverpool Canal **(A)**. Pass under a railway bridge and at a swing bridge, turn left over it to the main road. Turn right and at a public footpath sign, turn left to descend to the edge of a field. Turn right and follow the field edge to the left, keeping by a drain – the Rufford Boundary Sluice – on the right and passing through a vehicle yard to a lane.

Turn right over a bridge and turn left along a narrow path, now with the drain on the left. At a road turn left over a bridge, turn right to continue now with the drain on the right again, and at the next road turn right over a bridge. Turn left through a metal gate to continue, at first, along the left edge of Rufford Cricket Ground and later a field, with the drain once more on the left. In the field corner go through a kissing gate and turn right onto a path that keeps by the right inside edge of the beautiful woodlands of Mere Sands Wood Nature Reserve.

The path, which soon becomes more clearly defined and better surfaced, keeps close to the meandering edge of the woodland to reach a track to the right of the Nature Reserve car park and visitor centre **(B)**. Turn right over a stile and along the track to a road, turn right and at a public bridleway sign, turn left onto a track that keeps along the left edge of the woodlands of Rufford Park. To the left are wide, open views across flat country looking towards the coast.

At a crossroads follow the well-surfaced main track to the right, pass between farm buildings and continue along the left edge of woodland to reach the main road again by the Rufford Arms Hotel. Cross over, keep ahead along Spark Lane to a T-junction and turn right over the canal bridge. Turn left down steps to rejoin the canal, turn left under the bridge and follow the towpath back to Rufford.

On this last stage of the walk there are more extensive views to the left across flat country to the westerly edge of the Pennines on the horizon, and towards the end come glimpses on the right of Rufford Old Hall **(C)** through the trees on the opposite bank of the canal. After passing under a road bridge, turn sharp left up to the road, turn right and walk over a level crossing to return to the start.

Features of Interest

(A) This is the Rufford Branch of the Leeds-Liverpool Canal, constructed in 1805 to provide a link between the main canal and the Ribble estuary. For most of its length it runs roughly parallel to the River Douglas.

(B) Mere Sands Wood Nature Reserve, 105 acres of woodland, heath and lakes, is owned and managed by the Lancashire Wildlife Trust. It was originally an area of sand and peat on the edge of a large lake – Martin Mere – and after the lake was drained, Lord Hesketh of nearby Rufford planted the woodlands around the middle of the 19th century. Sand quarrying took place between 1974 and 1982. After completion, the extracted areas became shallow lakes and the site was acquired as a nature reserve. After looking around the Visitor Centre, you may wish to extend the walk by exploring further.

(C) One of the finest late medieval buildings in Lancashire, Rufford

Old Hall was the home of the Hesketh family who played a prominent role in the drainage schemes of the 18th and 19th centuries that transformed much of the surrounding barren mosses and marshland into fertile arable land. The original timber-framed building was subsequently enlarged but the Heskeths abandoned it in favour of a new hall, on the other side of the main road and which is now a hospital. In 1936, the original building was given to the National Trust. The most prominent feature of the interior is the superb Great Hall with its large screen and magnificent hammerbeam roof. There are also fine collections of paintings, furniture and armour and pleasant grounds beside the canal. Access is from the main A59.

22. Rivington Country Park

Start/Parking: Lever Park, Great House Barn — grid reference 628139.

Distance: 7 miles (11.3km).

Category: Moderate.

Refreshments: Café at Great House Barn.

Terrain: Combination of woodland, grassland and moorland, most of the paths and tracks are well-waymarked and well-surfaced but likely to be some muddy stretches, easy climb to Rivington Pike.

OS Maps: Landranger 109, Explorer 19.

Public transport: None, apart from an irregular bus service that runs through the park during the summer months. Buses from Preston, Chorley and Bolton pass the Horwich entrance to the park.

What you'll discover

The woodland, grassland and gardens of Rivington Country Park, situated beside Rivington Reservoirs and rising up to the slopes of Rivington Pike and the moorlands beyond, provide excellent walking facilities. In addition, Rivington village with its two churches, two ancient barns, Lord Leverhulme's terraced gardens and the mock ruins of Liverpool Castle create considerable historic interest, as this varied and absorbing walk clearly reveals. From the highest point, the 1191ft (361m) summit of Rivington Pike, the views are both extensive and superb.

Route Directions

Facing the road, take the path to the left of Great House Barn **(A)**, sign-posted Rivington, that runs roughly parallel with the road and joins it on the edge of the village. Turn left beside the village green **(B)** and, at a T-junction, turn left again and follow the road down to the reservoirs.

In front of the causeway between Upper and Lower Rivington Reservoirs **(C)**, turn right onto a tarmac track which bears right away from the water, bears right again and descends to cross a stream. Go through a kissing gate, walk along a tree-lined track, later heading uphill along the left edge of Dean Wood Nature Reserve, and climb a stile. Turn right along the edge of a field, climb a stile, continue along an enclosed path above a wooded ravine and go through a kissing gate onto a lane.

Turn left, turn right over a ladder stile and walk across a field to climb another ladder stile. Continue along the right edge of a field, by a stream on the right, climb a stile and then a ladder stile and keep ahead, by a fence – later a wall – on the left. At a ladder stile on the left, follow the directions of a waymark to the right and a follow a track through a gate onto a road. Turn left, heading gently uphill, and where the road bends left, turn right over a ladder stile.

Descend to climb a stile and cross a footbridge over a stream; bear right and head up to climb another stile. Continue across the grassy moorland – there are boardwalks in places – over several stiles and footbridges, eventually reaching a parking area. At the T-junction just beyond, turn left, at a 'Concessionary Bridleway' post, and take the right-hand one of two tracks ahead, passing through two gates. By a West Pennine Moors notice board, turn left up steps, climb a stile and follow a stepped path uphill, bending right towards the Pigeon Tower **(D)**. Keep to the left of the tower and climb a stile onto a track.

Turn right along the top edge of the Terraced Gardens and at a kissing gate, bear left and follow a track up steps to the tower on the summit of Rivington Pike **(E)**. From here turn right along a path that descends steeply to a track and continue along it, curving right to go through a gate. Cross a track, go through a kissing gate and follow a winding downhill path, passing through several gates. The path becomes a concrete track that bends sharply right and continues downhill. Just after a left curve, turn right onto a broad, straight track.

Keep along it for about half a mile and just after passing a house on the left, you reach a crossroads in front of a gate. Turn left down a tarmac track to a road, cross over and continue along the straight

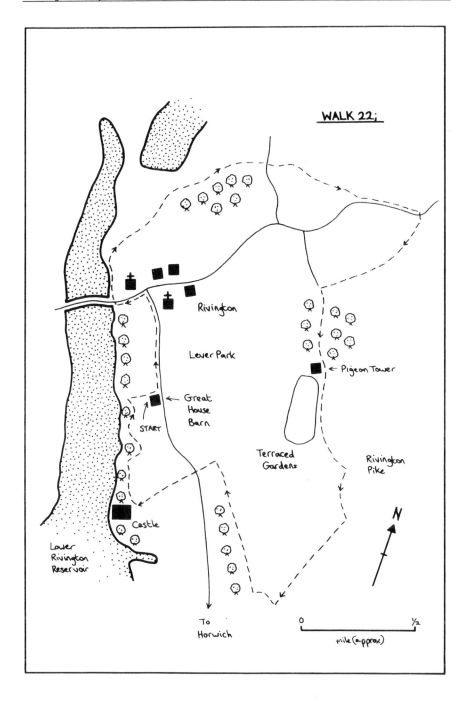

WALK 22;

Rivington

Lever Park

Pigeon Tower

Great
House
Barn

START

Terraced
Gardens

Rivington
Pike

N

Castle

Lower
Rivington
Reservoir

To
Horwich

0   ½

mile (approx)

track opposite, sign-posted 'Bridleway – Castle'. Turn right at a T-junction and to the left is the replica of the ruins of Liverpool Castle **(F)**.

Now follow a track, which winds along the right edge of the trees bordering the reservoir. Where the track turns right towards the road, keep ahead through trees to a fence corner and continue beside the reservoir, still keeping along the right edge of woodland. When you see Great House Barn over to the right, turn right and head across to return to the starting point.

Features of Interest

(A) Great House Barn is now a country park information centre and café. It is one of two ancient barns in the park; the other is Hall Barn, now a bar and restaurant, about half a mile to the north-east. Next to the latter is the 18th-century Rivington Hall, former home of the lords of the manor, the Pilkingtons, also a restaurant. Both barns were restored by Lord Leverhulme, who transformed the whole area after he acquired the estate in 1900. This remarkable man, born in Bolton in 1851, was one of the great capitalists of the Victorian era, building up a profitable soap empire from small beginnings in Warrington. He was also a philanthropist and established the model factory village of Port Sunlight on the Wirral for his workers. At Rivington, he created Lever Park as a public park for the enjoyment of the people of his home town of Bolton, constructing broad drives and planting thousands of trees. For himself he had the ornamental Terraced Gardens laid out around his bungalow on the upper slopes of Rivington Pike. After his death in 1925, both the park and gardens became neglected and overgrown but have been largely restored since becoming a country park. As a result, the park still fulfils the intentions of its founder as a much used recreational area.

(B) On opposite sides of the village green are the 16th-century church and small 18th-century Unitarian chapel.

(C) Both Upper and Lower Rivington Reservoirs were constructed by Liverpool Corporation around the middle of the 19th century.

(D) Lord Leverhulme built the Pigeon Tower as a dovecote. Nearby is the entrance to the Terraced Gardens, laid out by Lord Leverhulme in the Japanese style with fountains, lakes and waterfalls. The bungalow in which he lived was burnt down by suffragettes in 1913, subsequently rebuilt but demolished after falling into ruin after his death. The gardens are well worth an exploration and there are plans to restore them to their former glory.

(E) The contrasting views from Rivington Pike extend over the bare and bleak Rivington and Anglezarke Moors and the flat arable lands of the West Lancashire coastal plain. On clear days the mountains of the Lake District and Snowdonia can be seen from here. The tower was erected in 1773.

(F) These sham ruins, which occupy a fine position overlooking Lower Rivington reservoir, were built by Lord Leverhulme as a supposed replica of Liverpool Castle. (See Walk 29)

Great House Barn

23. Turton Tower and Last Drop Village

Start/Parking: Jumbles Country Park, Waterfold car park – grid reference 736140.

Distance: 7½ miles (12.1km).

Category: Moderate.

Refreshments: Kiosk (restricted opening) at Jumbles Information Centre at start, tea-room at Turton Tower, pub and tea shop at Last Drop Village, King William pub nearly half a mile south of Turton Tower.

Terrain: Mixture of water authority tracks, field paths and open moorland, most of the route is clear and well-defined.

OS Maps: Landranger 109, Explorer 19.

Public transport: Buses from Bolton, Rawtenstall and Bury pass the entrance to the Country Park.

What you'll discover

Jumbles Country Park, which is based around a reservoir, Turton Tower and Last Drop Village are the main focal points on this route. In between there is a varied mixture of waterside and moorland walking, with fine, panoramic views that extend from the Rossendale valley and West Pennine Moors across the built up area of Greater Manchester to the northern edge of the Peak District.

Route Directions

Begin by taking the track northwards along the east side of Jumbles Reservoir **(A)** and soon after the reservoir narrows, turn left and cross a bridge over it. Go up some steps and walk through trees to a stile, climb it and continue over the brow of a hill to climb another stile onto a road.

Turn left and turn right along the drive to Turton Tower **(B)**, passing in front of the house. Cross the railway bridge **(C)** and at a T-junction, turn right onto a track which you follow across open country for nearly 1½ miles to a road. Just before the road, turn left along a path that continues across grassy moorland, by the remains of a fence on the right, to a stile. Climb it, turn right and head across to climb another stile by a wall corner.

Turn left and continue steadily uphill, initially by a wall on the left and later going through a wall gap. Keep above a steep drop on the right and the path descends, by a wall on the left, to a convergence of walls at a field corner. Climb a stile, walk towards a farm and climb another stile to the left of the farm buildings. Continue along a track, climb a stile to the left of a gate and bear left along the left edge of a field. Climb another stile, cross a track, climb the stile opposite and turn left along the left edge of a field, heading towards the next farm. Climb two more stiles and keep to the left of the farmhouse to go through a gate.

Turton Tower

Continue along a track, climb a stile and pass in front of a barn. Keep along the left edge of a field, following it to the right and continuing to a stile in the field corner. Climb it, walk along a track above a quarry on the right, go through a gap and keep along the right edge of a field, going through a wall gap on the right in the top corner.

Turn right for a brief detour into Last Drop Village **(D)**. Retrace your steps and continue by bearing left and heading slightly uphill

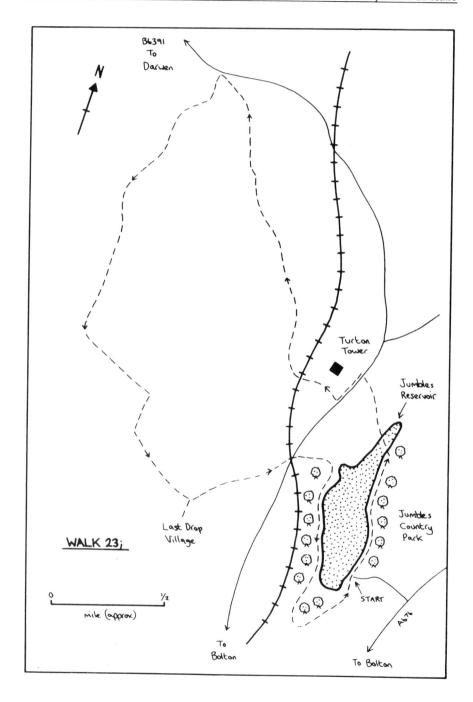

B6391
To
Darwen

N

Turton
Tower

Jumbles
Reservoir

Jumbles
Country
Park

Last Drop
Village

WALK 23;

0   1/2
mile (approx)

START

A676

To
Bolton

To Bolton

along the left edge of a field to a stile. Climb it, cross a track, climb the stile opposite and keep ahead, by a wall on the right. Cross a broken down wall in the field corner and continue for a few metres by a low wall on the right. At the wall corner, keep ahead to go through a metal gate and walk down a track to a road by the King William pub.

Turn left and, immediately after passing under a railway bridge, turn right at a footpath sign; thrn, cross a track and climb a stile. Continue downhill across a field, keeping to the left of the buildings ahead, go through a gate and continue across a paved track to join another track. Bear right along it, turn right over a bridge and walk along the west side of the reservoir.

Continue along a tree-lined avenue and, at a footpath sign to Jumbles Reservoir, turn left over a stile. Walk along a path, climb another stile and cross a footbridge below a dam. Finally, climb a flight of steps to return to the start.

Features of Interest

(A) Jumbles Reservoir, built in 1971, is one of a series constructed in the Bradshaw valley to the north of Bolton. The land around it was created a country park in 1973.

(B) Originally a simple, 15th-century pele tower built to repel Scottish invaders, Turton Tower was enlarged and remodelled in the late 16th century and again in the Victorian period to become a comfortable family home. Much of the fine panelling and antique furniture came from nearby demolished houses.

(C) The 19th-century railway bridge that spans the Blackburn-Bolton line was adorned with battlements in order to make it harmonise with Turton Tower.

(D) Last Drop Village is a collection of old farm buildings, restored and converted into a traditional English village in the 1960s by a local businessman. It includes a hotel, pub, tea shop, galleries and craft and antique shops.

24. Blackstone Edge

Start/Parking: Car park on A58 just below White House pub and Blackstone Edge reservoir — grid reference 967178.

Distance: 4½ miles (7.2km).

Category: Moderate.

Refreshments: White House pub at start.

Terrain: Rough moorland tracks, steady rather than steep climb up the Roman road but the short stretch along the Pennine Way to the trig point on the summit is likely to be soggy, avoid in bad weather and poor visibility.

OS Maps: Landranger 109, Outdoor Leisure 21.

Public transport: Buses from Rochdale and Halifax.

What you'll discover

From below it is easy to see how Blackstone Edge acquired its name, as even in sunny conditions the grit-stone rocks at the summit look dark and forbidding. The highlight of this walk, high up on the windy and exposed slopes of the Pennines, is a climb along part of an ancient routeway, thought to be a Roman road, onto the edge, a magnificent viewpoint overlooking the moors, Rochdale and the built up area of Greater Manchester.

Route Directions

From the car park turn right onto a track, at a public bridleway sign, which heads steadily downhill, keeping roughly parallel with the road. Just after passing to the right of a pool, the track bears left to re-join the main road opposite a cottage.

Continue along the lane opposite (Blackstone Edge Old Road) into the hamlet of Lydgate and shortly after crossing a stream, turn

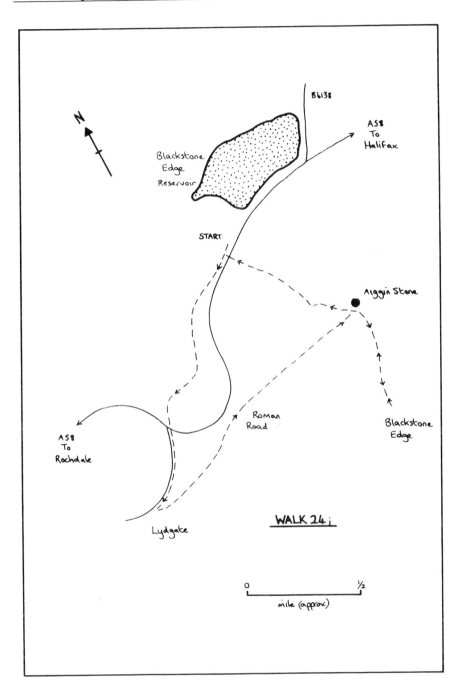

N

B6138

A58
To
Halifax

Blackstone
Edge
Reservoir

START

Aiggin Stone

A58
To
Rochdale

Roman
Road

Blackstone
Edge

Lydgate

WALK 24 i

0   ½

mile (approx)

sharp left onto a track, at a public footpath sign to Blackstone Edge. Pass in front of a row of cottages and continue uphill, alongside a wall on the right. The distinctive rocks on Blackstone Edge can be seen on the horizon immediately ahead. After crossing a track, the ascent becomes steeper and the stones that mark the line of the Roman road become more clearly exposed **(A)**. A particularly impressive stretch appears after crossing a drainage channel.

Continue up to a cairn and the Aiggin Stone, the latter probably an old guide post, where the Pennine Way crosses the Roman road. Turn right through a kissing gate and follow the Pennine Way across the rough, peaty moorland and between boulders to the trig point at the summit **(B)**.

Retrace your steps to the Roman road, cross it and keep ahead along the Pennine Way – the route is reasonably well-defined – descending to the drainage channel crossed previously. Look out for where you cross it via a concrete footbridge and turn right alongside it as far as a gate. At a public footpath sign in front of the gate, the path turns left and heads down to the start.

Features of Interest

(A) Although this broad, stone causeway is always referred to as the Roman Road – and named as such on Ordnance Survey maps – there is some doubt as to whether its origins are Roman or later. However it is certainly an ancient routeway and one of the most impressive in the country, with wheel grooves and a drainage channel clearly visible.

(B) The views from the 1550ft (470m) summit extend over the surrounding moorland and overlook Littleborough, Rochdale and much of Greater Manchester. Immediately below is Hollingworth Lake, originally built in 1778 to supply water to the Rochdale Canal. In Victorian times it became a popular weekend resort and is now the focal point of a country park.

25. Manchester

Start: Piccadilly.

Parking: Manchester.

Distance: 4 miles (6.4km).

Category: Easy.

Refreshments: Plenty of places to eat and drink in Manchester.

Terrain: Easy town walking.

Maps: Pick up a street map from the Visitor Information Centre in St Peter's Square.

Public transport: Manchester is served by buses and trains from all the surrounding towns and has coach and rail links with all parts of the country.

What you'll discover

Manchester has been described as the first industrial city. Originally a small Roman fort, it grew rapidly in the late 18th and early 19th centuries when it became the commercial centre of the flourishing cotton industry. It continued to develop into one of the great trading and manufacturing cities of the world, even becoming a major port after the construction of the Manchester Ship Canal in 1898 linked it to the Mersey estuary. This walk around the city centre enables you to see many of the commercial, civic and transport monuments to the city's Victorian greatness, as well as some earlier and later buildings. The greatest concentration of such monuments is at the Castlefield Urban Heritage Park, which also embraces the remains of the Roman fort of Mamucium, the birthplace of the city.

Route Directions

Start in Piccadilly on the north side of the gardens and turn right down Portland Street. Here and in the adjoining streets are some of the finest examples of the imposing 19th-century warehouses, now put to other uses, that symbolise the heyday of the cotton industry. They are considered by many to be the most distinctive feature of Manchester's architecture. The area to the right is also the city's Chinatown, with many Chinese businesses and restaurants.

Turn right into Princess Street and as you cross Mosley Street the City Art Gallery **(A)** is to the right. Keep ahead across St Peter's Square and along the right side of the Town Hall into Albert Square and turn left in front of the Town Hall **(B)**. Turn left again along Lloyd Street, passing under two bridges that link the Town Hall with a later extension, back into St Peter's Square. Turn right to pass the circular Central Library, opened in 1934, and in front of the Midland Hotel turn right along Peter Street as far as the Free Trade Hall **(C)**.

Walk along Southmill Street at the side of the Free Trade Hall to emerge in front of the G-Mex Centre; beyond it to the left is the modern Bridgewater Hall **(D)**. Following signs to Deansgate Station, take the covered walkway to the right of the G-Mex Centre, continue along the right edge of a car park to the G-Mex Metro station, cross the track, turn right and descend steps. Cross Deansgate, continue along Castle Street beside the Rochdale Canal and, after passing under a railway bridge, enter the Castlefield complex **(E)**.

Turn left down steps to the Bridgewater Canal, turn right over a metal footbridge and keep beside the canal, following it as it curves right. Climb steps to the Merchants Warehouse, built in 1825 and the oldest surviving warehouse in Castlefield, keep ahead to cross a bridge over the Rochdale Canal and bear left to the canal basin. Turn right under a brick railway viaduct, cross another canal bridge, and pass under two more adjacent viaducts. Descend steps, continue by an arm of the canal, passing under another brick viaduct, and walk across an open space to the base of some steps. Climb them onto Liverpool Road and turn right beside the Castlefield Centre.

Keep ahead to Collier Street to view the Roman fort; otherwise the route continues to the left along Lower Byrom Street. Walk between the Air and Space Gallery and the Museum of Science and Industry,

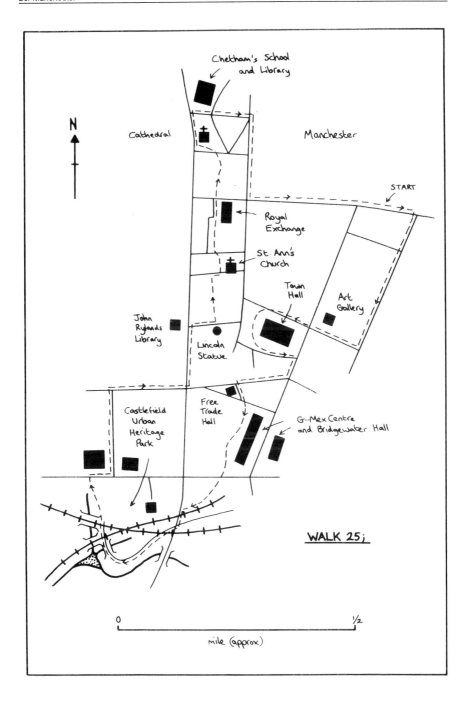

N

Chetham's School and Library

Cathedral

Manchester

START

Royal Exchange

St. Ann's Church

Town Hall

Art Gallery

John Rylands Library

Lincoln Statue

Castlefield Urban Heritage Park

Free Trade Hall

G-Mex Centre and Bridgewater Hall

WALK 25;

0   ½

mile (approx)

keep ahead to a T-junction – Granada Studios is to the left – and turn right along Quay Street. At a crossroads turn left into Deansgate and opposite the John Rylands Library **(F)**, turn right along Brazennose Street to the Lincoln Statue **(G)**.

Just past the statue turn left through an arcade to St Mary's Church, known as the 'Hidden Gem' because of its location and fine interior, turn left again and then right into Ridgefield. On reaching King Street, turn first right and then left through the covered St Ann's Passage to St Ann's Church **(H)**. Walk through St Ann's Square and keep ahead along Exchange Street, passing to the right of the Royal Exchange **(J)**, to St Mary's Gate. Continue along the passageway opposite, sign-posted Market Hall, into Shambles Square and to the right is Sinclairs and the Old Wellington Inn, two fine 16th-century timbered buildings. Turn right, then left and descend steps to Cateaton Street. Cross over and continue along Cathedral Gates to Manchester Cathedral **(K)**.

At the time of writing (1999) a lot of reconstruction work was still going on in this part of the city because of the IRA bomb. If the footpath between St Mary's Gate and Cateaton Street is closed, turn left along St Mary's Gate and turn right along Deansgate to the cathedral.

Walk in front of the cathedral, briefly rejoining Deansgate, and turn right into Fennel Street, passing to the right of Chetham's School and Library **(L)**. Turn right along Corporation Street, turn left under an arch about half way along the Arndale Centre and walk along Market Street back to Piccadilly.

Features of Interest

(A) This Grecian-style building was designed by Sir Charles Barry, later the architect of the Houses of Parliament, in 1823.

(B) Manchester Town Hall (1868-77) is one of the great civic monuments of Victorian England. It was built in a flamboyant Gothic style by Sir Alfred Waterhouse and its design was based on that of the medieval cloth halls of Flanders. The clock tower rises to 268ft. Inside are displayed many facets of the city's history.

The G-Mex Centre with the Bridgwater Hall in the background

(C) The present Renaissance-style hall dates from the 1850s but its predecessor was associated with the free trade movement of the early 19th century which was based in Manchester. In particular it was the home of the Anti-Corn League, an organisation dedicated to the removal of the high duties on imported corn at the time in order that food would be cheaper for ordinary people.

The Free Trade Hall also stands on the site of the infamous 'Peterloo Massacre' of August 1819. A large crowd, estimated at around 60,000, had gathered to hear speeches by Henry 'Orator' Hunt, a fiery radical leader. Fearing trouble, the authorities used military force to disperse them, leaving many dead or injured. 'Peterloo' is a sarcastic reference to another successful military victory four years earlier at Waterloo.

(D) The former Central Station was reopened in 1980, its centenary year, as the G-Mex Centre, an exhibition centre and indoor arena. On the other side of the road is the ultra-modern Bridgewater Hall, the new home of the Halle Orchestra.

(E) The collection of industrial and commercial buildings at Castlefield, grouped around a canal basin and criss-crossed by railway viaducts, is of unique interest. This was the terminus of the world's first commercial canal, the Bridgewater Canal, completed in 1765. It was also the terminus of the world's first regular passenger railway between Liverpool and Manchester, opened in 1830. After the Industrial Revolution, there followed a long period of decline and dereliction until 1982 when Castlefield was designated an urban heritage park. The resultant cleaning up and restoration has produced an attractive area of canalside walks and refurbished warehouses, with a good selection of pubs, restaurants and cafés. It is well worth a lengthy exploration and there are plenty of information boards scattered about. It is probably best to start at the Visitor Centre on Liverpool Road where there are displays and useful guides and leaflets.

Among the foremost attractions are the Air and Space Gallery, which occupies the former Lower Campfield market, an impressive Victorian glass and steel structure. Opposite is the Museum of Science and Industry, housed in the original station buildings of the Liverpool-Manchester Railway. The station became a goods depot after the establishment of Victoria Station in 1844.

It is perhaps ironic that Manchester's great industrial expansion began on the very site where the city originated. The Roman fort of Mamucium was built in 79 AD, rebuilt several times and finally abandoned in 410 AD. Around the fort, a later civilian settlement or 'vicus' grew up. The few visible remains are the foundations of the granary and part of the vicus, and there is a reconstruction of the North Gate of the fort.

(F) John Rylands was a local philanthropic textile manufacturer and this fine Victorian building was erected by his widow in the 1890s, both as a memorial to him and to house his collection of rare books.

(G) The statue of Abraham Lincoln was erected to commemorate the support given by the working people of Manchester to the abolition of slavery in the USA, even though the lack of imports of raw cotton during the American Civil War led to hardship and unemployment among textile workers. Lincoln later sent a letter of thanks, parts of which are inscribed on the base of the statue.

(H) This dignified church, on the south side of elegant St Ann's Square, was built in 1709.

(J) The Royal Exchange, built 1868-74, was the main international business centre of the cotton industry until it ceased trading in 1968. Since then it has been skilfully converted into a theatre in the round.

(K) This large, handsome, mainly 15th-century collegiate church was chosen as the cathedral when a new diocese of Manchester was created in 1848. The interior is particularly noted for the carvings on the late medieval choir stalls.

(L) Chetham's School and Library was founded by Humphrey Chetham in 1653 and housed in a former 15th-century manor house. The library claims to be the oldest free library in the world and among its many users were Marx and Engels. Later buildings were erected in 1870 for Manchester Grammar School but, since 1969, they have been used by Chetham's Music School.

26. Worsley and the Bridgewater Canal

Start/Parking: Worsley, car park on Barton Road opposite the Court House – grid reference 747004.

Distance: 3 miles (4.8km).

Category: Easy.

Refreshments: None.

Terrain: Flat and easy to follow walking along a canal towpath, disused railway line and woodland paths.

OS Maps: Landranger 109, Pathfinders 712 and 723.

Public transport: Buses from Manchester and Wigan.

What you'll discover

Although never out of earshot of the M62, this is a walk through a real rural basis that is full of interest as one of the key places in the development of the Industrial Revolution. Chief focal point is the Bridgewater Canal and the first part of the walk is along its towpath from Worsley to Monton Green. A later form of transport – a former railway line – is utilised for the return and the final stretch is a stroll through part of the extensive and attractive Worsley Woods. A series of useful 'Worsley Heritage' information boards line the route.

Route Directions

Turn right out of the car park and shortly bear left across grass to join the towpath of the Bridgewater Canal **(A)**. The large open space on the other side of the canal is Worsley Green. Continue along the towpath, heading up to the road at the first bridge.

Turn left over it into Monton Green and just before a road junction, turn left up a tarmac path and pass through a barrier to join a

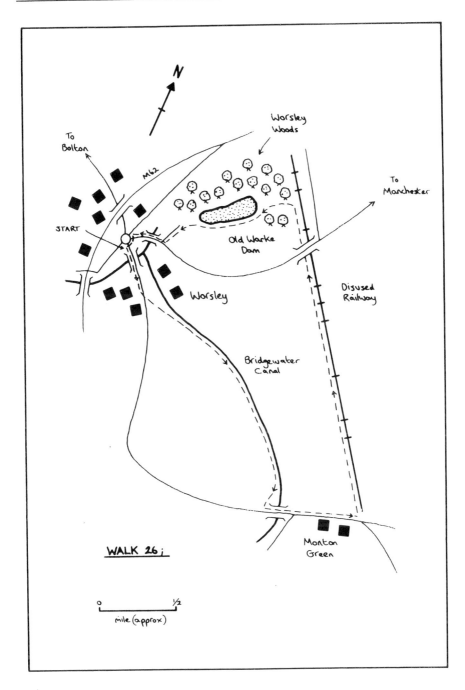

N

Worsley
Woods

To
Bolton

M62

To
Manchester

START

Old Warke
Dam

Worsley

Disused
Railway

Bridgewater
Canal

WALK 26 ;

Monton
Green

0   ½
mile (approx)

disused railway track **(B)** on the site of the former Monton Green station. Walk along the track - on top of a broad, straight, tree-lined embankment - and pass beside a gate to reach the site of the former Worsley station. Go under a bridge, pass beside another gate and continue along the track, now through a cutting, as far as flights of steps on both sides, about 20 metres before the next gate.

Turn left up the steps, go through a kissing gate and take the path ahead into Worsley Woods **(C)**. At a junction of paths, keep ahead, passing beside a barrier and along a path which passes to the left of a black and white house. The path continues, by a fence on the right, beside the edge of Old Warke Dam and eventually emerges from the woods at a gate.

Keep ahead down a lane, passing some attractive whitewashed cottages, to the main road and turn right to cross the canal bridge **(D)**. At a road junction turn left to return to the start.

The Bridgewater Canal at Worsley

Features of Interest

(A) The Bridgewater Canal was one of the earliest canals in the country and the first major canal of the Industrial Revolution era. Conceived by the 3rd Duke of Bridgewater and started by James Brindley in 1759, it was constructed to link the duke's coal mines at Worsley with Manchester. So successful was it – the price of coal in Manchester was halved – that it pioneered the great canal boom of the second half of the 18th century during which Brindley went on to build canals all over the country.

In the village are a number of attractive black and white buildings from the canal era. The Packet House, seen to the left along the canal, dates from 1760 although the black and white timbering was only added around 1850. Worsley Court House, opposite the car park, was built in the middle of the 19th century as the village hall but was later used as a magistrates' court.

(B) The line, opened in 1864 and closed in 1969, ran between Wigan and Eccles. Since the 1980s it has been developed to form part of the Tyldesley Loopline, a well-used recreational route.

(C) Worsley Woods were planted in the middle of the 19th century by the Earl of Ellesmere, using redundant local coal miners.

(D) The rock face seen to the right is the Delph. From here emerged the underground canals which went deep into the Duke of Bridgewater's mines.

27. Haigh Hall and Wigan Pier

Start/Parking: Haigh Hall Country Park – grid reference 596085.

Distance: 8 miles (12.9km).

Category: Moderate.

Refreshments: Stables Café at Haigh Hall, pubs and cafés in Wigan town centre, Orwell pub and restaurant and the Pantry Café at the Wigan Pier complex, Kirkless Hall pub near Top Lock.

Terrain: Flat and easy walking mainly along tarmac drives and canal towpaths, with the middle part of the route passing through Wigan town centre.

OS Maps: Landrangers 108 and 109, Pathfinders 711 and 712.

Public transport: The walk could be started from the centre of Wigan which is served by buses all the surrounding towns. Wigan also has two railway stations: Wallgate is on the Manchester-Southport line and North Western is on the main west coast route from London to Glasgow via Stafford, Crewe and Warrington, and on to Preston, Lancaster and Carlisle.

What you'll discover

A walk full of interest and variety which starts and finishes in the delightfully wooded surroundings of Haigh Hall Country Park and takes you, via Wigan town centre, to the nationally renowned Wigan Pier heritage site. Considering the proximity of Wigan, the landscape is remarkably green and unspoilt. One reason for this is that the route makes use of the 'green corridors' of the River Douglas and the Leeds-Liverpool Canal to enter and leave the town centre. Another reason is that this is now a largely post-industrial landscape. It has been reclaimed from the previous industrial squalor and dereliction for which the area used to be notorious. Allow plenty of time to enjoy the Wigan Pier experience.

Wigan Pier

Route Directions

The walk begins on the terrace of Haigh Hall **(A)**, overlooking Wigan and the Douglas valley. Turn right by the side of the hall, turn left in front of a flight of steps and follow a drive up to the entrance gates to the country park. Turn left along a lane and just after reaching a group of trees on the left, turn left again onto a sunken track.

The track winds downhill to a bridge over the Leeds-Liverpool Canal. Cross the bridge, turn left down steps to the towpath and keep along it as far as the next bridge, number 60. In front of the bridge turn right up steps and turn right along a drive that winds through the Haigh Lower Plantations **(B)**. After a sharp right bend, you join a stream on the left and just before bearing right to a bridge over the River Douglas, turn left down steps to cross a footbridge over the stream.

Turn right up steps on the other side and continue through woodland above the river. The path becomes a tarmac track, which descends to cross the Douglas and reach a lane. Take the tarmac track opposite which continues along the right bank of the river, passes under a road bridge, keeps alongside Central Park, the home of Wigan Rugby League club, and emerges onto a road on the edge of Wigan town centre. Keep ahead, at traffic lights turn left along Standishgate and walk through the heart of the shopping centre, passing through the Market Place and continuing along Wallgate. Go under a railway bridge by North Western station and keep ahead to meet the Leeds-Liverpool canal again by the Wigan Pier complex **(C)**.

Join a canalside path opposite Trencherfield Mill, descend a cobbled path, turn left under a bridge, opposite the Orwell Pub and Restaurant, and walk along the towpath, passing in front of the huge Trencherfield Mill. Continue along the towpath for the next 3½ miles, a perhaps surprisingly green and pleasant walk considering its proximity to Wigan town centre. The first part is called the Promenade, recently paved and attractively landscaped. The route passes by the long Wigan Flight of Locks to reach Top Lock where the canal does a left bend. On the way look out on the left for Peel Hall **(D)** and a bit further on the distinctive 'Rabbit Rocks' **(E)** on the right.

Keep along the towpath to bridge no 60 again. Here bear left up steps, turn right over the bridge and follow a drive through the Upper Plantations **(F)**. The drive curves left to return to Haigh Hall.

Features of Interest

(A) Haigh Hall, built in the 19th century near the site of an earlier house, belonged to the Earls of Crawford who owned an iron foundry and coal mines in the vicinity. In 1947, both the hall and surrounding grounds were sold to Wigan Corporation; the hall is used for functions and the well-wooded grounds are now an attractive and popular country park. The former stables and coach house now accommodate a shop, exhibition area and café.

(B) These fine woodlands were planted by the Earl of Crawford in the early 19th century.

(C) The Leeds-Liverpool Canal played a major role in the industrial development of Wigan and the surrounding area. It was originally

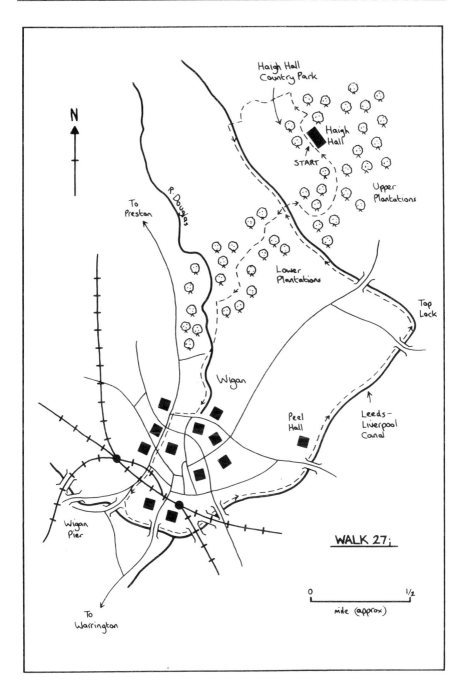

N

Haigh Hall
Country Park

Haigh
Hall

START

Upper
Plantations

To
Preston

R. Douglas

Lower
Plantations

Top
Lock

Wigan

Peel
Hall

Leeds–
Liverpool
Canal

Wigan
Pier

WALK 27;

To
Warrington

0   ½
mile (approx)

opened between Liverpool and Wigan in 1781. By 1816 the completion of the connection with Leeds meant that Wigan was now linked with the Mersey, the Ribble, Manchester, the Lancashire cotton towns, and across the Pennines to Leeds and the Yorkshire woollen towns. The actual 'Wigan Pier', source of the music hall joke, is a rather unimpressive coal staithe opposite the main exhibition building, from which coal was tipped into the waiting barges.

Canal traffic inevitably declined but the music hall joke, allegedly invented by George Formby senior, has developed into a most fascinating and imaginative industrial heritage site. Chief attraction is 'The Way We Were' exhibition, housed in a restored warehouse. This is an attempt to recreate everyday life in Wigan in 1900: in the mines and mills, shops and pubs, at school and on a trip to the seaside. A short distance away is Trencherfield Mill where you can see the world's largest original mill steam engine in action, plus many other machines. The complex also includes a pub and restaurant, shop, children's play area and canal-side gardens. Although on the route, the brief journey from 'The Way We Were' site to Trencherfield Mill can be made via one of the regular waterbuses if you wish, all part of the overall enjoyment of a visit to Wigan Pier.

(D) This is a rare surviving example in this area of a medieval house. The oldest parts date from the 14th century.

(E) Rabbit Rocks is a local nickname for the waste tips from the former Kirkless Iron and Steel Works which once occupied a huge area beside the canal. It closed down in 1931 at the height of the Great Depression.

(F) Workers made unemployed by the Cotton Famine, caused by the cessation of imports of raw cotton from the Deep South during the American Civil War, were used in the planting of these additional woods in the 1860s.

28. Formby Point

Start/Parking: Formby Point, National Trust car park – grid reference 274083.

Distance: 5 miles (8km).

Category: Easy.

Refreshments: None.

Terrain: Mixture of sand dunes, pine woods and beach, with a small amount of suburban walking.

OS Maps: Landranger 108, Pathfinder 710.

Public transport: The walk could be started from Freshfield station which is served by trains from Liverpool and Southport and a local circular bus service from Formby.

What you'll discover

This bracing and exhilarating walk takes you across the dunes and through the attractive pine woods at Formby Point, owned by the National Trust. It includes part of the Ainsdale Dunes National Nature Reserve, noted for its varied and interesting flora and fauna. The last half mile is along a stretch of the flat and wide beaches that are characteristic of this part of the Merseyside coast.

Route Directions

Facing the sea, turn right and take the yellow-waymarked track that leads off from the car park, sign-posted Sefton Coastal Footpath **(A)**. Soon after the track curves right, a waymarked post directs you to the left to continue along a sandy path across the dunes. After passing an Ainsdale Dunes National Nature Reserve notice board, the path bears right away from the dunes and beach to a meeting of paths.

Turn right, still following Sefton Coastal Footpath signs, to join the Fisherman's Path **(B)**, a most attractive part of the route that continues through the pinewoods of the nature reserve. On the far side of the woods, keep ahead to pass beside a gate, continue across part of Formby golf course, cross the railway line and turn right onto a track alongside it. The track becomes a tarmac drive and continues, between houses on the left and the railway line on the right, to a road by Freshfield station.

Turn right over a level crossing and take the first turning on the left – College Path. Where the lane bends left, pass through the barrier ahead, at a public footpath sign to Blundell Avenue, and bear right along a tree-lined tarmac path to a road. Keep ahead along Firs Link and after crossing St Peter's Avenue, the route continues straight ahead along a paved path, crossing a succession of quiet, suburban roads.

At Larkhill Lane you leave the houses behind and keep ahead along a tarmac drive – Blundell Avenue – through woodland. Where the drive turns left, keep ahead (passing a Formby Point National Trust sign) along a path through trees. There are several path junctions here but keep on the main path all the while – the way is marked by a series of short posts – to emerge onto the dunes again.

In front of a Blundell Path sign, bear slightly right over the dunes and at the next footpath sign, keep ahead, in the Beach direction, over more dunes and descend to the beach. Turn right along the edge of it as far as a marker post to Victoria Road North. Turn right and head over the dunes once more to return to the car park.

Features of Interest

(A) Around 500 acres of coastline, sand dunes and pine woods at Formby Point are owned by the National Trust, part of one of the finest dune systems in England which stretches from Liverpool to Southport. Through it threads the well-waymarked Sefton Coastal Footpath.

(B) Now a popular recreational route, the Fisherman's Path is an old right of way by which the local fishermen used to make their way to

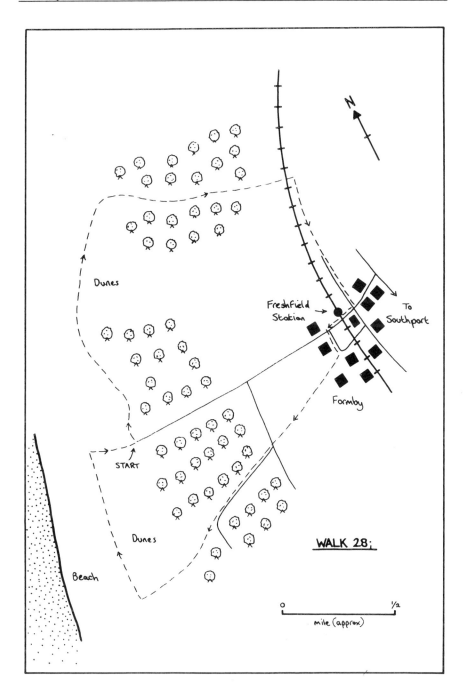

the shore. It runs through the pine woods of the Ainsdale Dunes National Nature Reserve, established in 1965 to protect the interesting and rare plants and animals found here. These include dune helleborine orchids, sand lizards, natterjack toads and red squirrels. The trees, mainly Corsican pines, were planted around 100 years ago to help stabilise the dunes.

Dunes and pine woods at Formby Point

29. Liverpool

Start: Pier Head.

Parking: Liverpool, Albert Dock.

Distance: 4 miles (6.4km).

Category: Easy.

Refreshments: Plenty of places to eat and drink in Liverpool.

Terrain: Easy town walking.

Maps: Pick up a street map from the Tourist Information Centre at Albert Dock.

Public transport: Liverpool is served by buses and trains from all the surrounding trains and has coach and rail links with all parts of the country.

What you'll discover

Liverpool is a maritime city with one of the best known and most distinguished waterfronts in the world. It grew rapidly from around the middle of the 18th century, trading extensively in sugar, tobacco, slaves and especially cotton with the West Indian and American colonies. As the Lancashire cotton industry expanded during the Industrial Revolution, most of the imported raw material and exported finished products passed through Liverpool. In the 19th century it also became an important passenger port and millions of emigrants sailed from here to seek a new life in the New World. Liverpool is generally regarded as possessing the most impressive collection of Victorian public buildings of any provincial city in Britain and has two contrasting modern cathedrals. In the 1960s it acquired additional fame as the birthplace of the Beatles, which has given the city a permanent niche in the annals of popular music. Although no longer a great port, its maritime heritage survives in the splendidly restored Albert Dock, a major tourist attraction. All these varied attractions and facets of the city's history are combined on this walk, plus fine views across the Mersey estuary.

Route Directions

The walk begins at the Pier Head beside the Albert Dock complex **(A)**, whose varied attractions are probably best saved until the end of the walk. With your back to the River Mersey, turn left to walk in front of the trio of imposing buildings that make up the Liverpool Waterfront **(B)** and turn right at the end of the Royal Liver Building. Ahead is St Nicholas' church **(C)**. Turn right again and turn left along Water Street to the Town Hall **(D)**.

Continue past it, turn right into North John Street and turn left along Victoria Street to emerge in front of the group of Victorian civic monuments dominated by St George's Hall. Cross the road, go up steps and walk through St John's Gardens, passing to the left of St George's Hall **(E)**. Turn right along Lime Street in front of the hall, follow the road as it bears left and on reaching the Britannia Adelphi Hotel, bear left up Mount Pleasant – some good brick terraces here – to the Roman Catholic cathedral **(F)**.

Retrace your steps down Mount Pleasant and turn left along Rodney Street, one of the most elegant streets in the city with some fine Georgian terraces. William Gladstone was born in 1809 at number 62. At the end of the street, the massive Anglican cathedral **(G)** rears above you. In front of the cathedral turn right down Upper Duke Street and turn right along Berry Street. Here you are on the edge of Liverpool's Chinatown, the oldest established Chinese community in Europe.

Opposite the war-damaged St Luke's church, turn left along Bold Street, passing the Lyceum Library and Newsroom **(H)**. Continue along the pedestrianised Church Street through the heart of the shopping centre and a brief detour to the left along Church Alley brings you to the Bluecoat Chambers **(J)**.

A little further along Church Street turn right into Whitechapel and turn left into Button Street to enter the Cavern Quarter **(K)**. Then turn left into Mathew Street, passing the site of the legendary Cavern

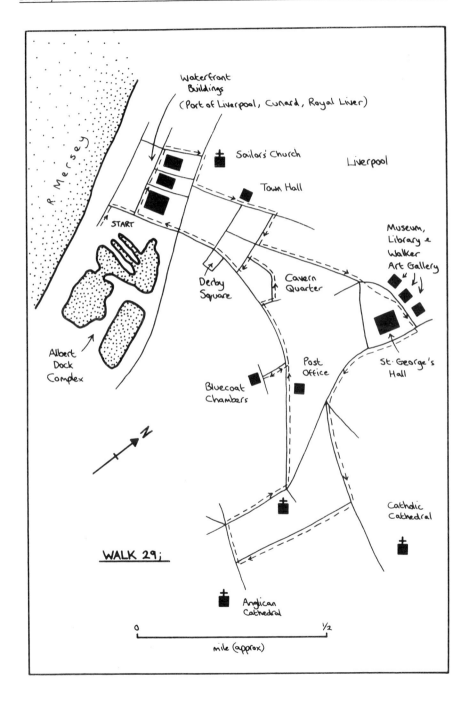

R. Mersey

Waterfront
Buildings
(Port of Liverpool, Cunard, Royal Liver)

Sailors' Church

Liverpool

Town Hall

START

Derby
Square

Cavern
Quarter

Museum,
Library &
Walker
Art Gallery

Albert
Dock
Complex

Bluecoat
Chambers

Post
Office

St. George's
Hall

N

Catholic
Cathedral

WALK 29;

Anglican
Cathedral

0   ½

mile (approx)

Club, to emerge into North John Street. Turn left, turn right along Lord Street, cross Derby Square **(L)** and continue down James Street. Keep ahead over Strand Street to return to the Pier Head.

And why not round off the walk by taking a 'Ferry Cross the Mersey' for the best views of all of the stunning waterfront and the city's skyline dominated by the two cathedrals?

Albert Dock, Liverpool

Features of Interest

(A) You could spend all day at the Albert Dock as there is so much to see. Designed by Jesse Hartley and opened by Prince Albert in 1846, the dock was the hub of the port of Liverpool in the Victorian era. The demise of the sailing ships began the process of decline and it finally closed in 1972. After lying derelict, these handsome buildings were restored and reopened in 1984 and have become a hub again – not of commercial but of recreational and cultural activities.

The major attractions within the complex are the Museum of Liverpool Life, the fascinating Merseyside Maritime Museum, the Tate Gallery of 20th-century art, and the Beatles Story which attempts to recreate the sights, sounds and atmosphere of the 'Swinging Sixties' when Liverpool was the pop music capital of the world. In addition there are shops, pubs, restaurants and cafés.

(B) All three buildings are roughly contemporary, built just before the First World War and symbolising Liverpool's confidence and prosperity at the time. The first is the Port of Liverpool Building, completed in 1907 to serve as the administrative headquarters of the port. Next is the Cunard Building (1916), formerly the headquarters of the Cunard Steamship Company. Last, and possibly the best known and most impressive, is the Royal Liver Building. Opened in 1911, it rises 322ft above the Mersey, topped by the mythical Liver Birds.

(C) This is commonly known as the Sailors' Church and there has been a church on the site since at least the 14th century.

(D) Most of Britain's great provincial cities have Victorian town halls but Liverpool's is Georgian, built between 1749 and 1754 by John Wood the Elder, famed as the architect of much of Bath's splendid Georgian heritage. After fire damage in 1795, the two-storey portico and dome were added by James Wyatt.

(E) St George's Hall has been described as the greatest neo-Classical building in the world and Queen Victoria proclaimed that it was 'worthy of ancient Athens'. It was the work of two architects – Elmes designed it and Cockerell completed it – and was built between 1842 and 1854. To the left, lining William Brown Street, are more grand Classical public buildings erected in the second half of the 19th century: the Liverpool Museum, Central Library and Walker Art Gallery.

(F) The Roman Catholic Cathedral was designed by Sir Frederick Gibberd and opened in 1967. It is much less traditional than its Anglican neighbour, built of concrete and circular in shape with a corona rising above the centre.

(G) Whether viewing Liverpool Cathedral from a distance or close up, or walking round the vast and uncluttered interior, adjectives like overwhelming and majestic immediately spring to mind. Guide books are full of superlatives: the largest Anglican church in the world and the largest cathedral in Britain with the largest organ and heaviest ring of bells. Built from local sandstone, it stands in a commanding position overlooking the city and river. The architect was Sir Giles Gilbert Scott. Work began in 1904 but the interruptions of two world wars delayed its completion until 1978.

(H) Now the post office, this dignified Classical structure was built by Thomas Harrison in 1800-02 to house what is alleged to be the first lending library in Europe.

(J) This elegant, early 18th-century building, oldest in the city centre, was originally a charity school. It is now a centre for art and crafts.

(K) The area around the legendary Cavern Club attracts devotees of the Beatles from all over the world. It has now been transformed into the Cavern Walks Shopping Centre, with coffee shops, pubs and restaurants. The site of the Cavern Club is in Mathew Street and opposite is the Cavern Pub whose 'Wall of Fame', unveiled in 1997, features the names, inscribed on bricks, of every band or group that performed at the Cavern between its opening in 1957 and its closure in 1973.

(L) Derby Square, dominated by a monument to Queen Victoria, occupies the site of the 13th-century castle which was totally demolished in 1721. Lord Leverhulme had a supposed replica of the castle ruins built in Lever Park near Bolton. (See Walk 22).

30. Croxteth Hall and Country Park

Start/Parking: Croxteth Country Park – grid reference 405942.

Distance: 3 miles (4.8km).

Category: Easy.

Refreshments: Café near Croxteth Hall.

Terrain: Flat and well-surfaced route, much of it on tarmac paths, across parkland and through woodland.

OS Maps: Landranger 108, Pathfinder 722.

Public transport: Buses from Liverpool city centre pass the entrance to the Country Park.

What you'll discover

Apart from some traffic noise and glimpses of modern houses in places, it is difficult to believe that this walk is only a few miles from the centre of Liverpool. The route is basically a circuit of the grounds surrounding Croxteth Hall, now a country park, an attractive mixture of formal gardens, woodland and grassland, with a brief stretch beside the infant River Alt. Inevitably the focal point is the hall itself, formerly the home of the Earls of Sefton, together with its gardens and adjoining farm. The tour of the hall provides you with a good insight into the workings of a great country house and its estate when such places were at their height in the period just before the First World War.

Route Directions

Start by taking the path that leads off from the far end of the car park which bears right and descends a few steps to a T-junction. Turn left onto a tarmac track, in the 'Hall, Farm and Gardens' direction, pass under a rather elaborate bridge that takes the track under Croxteth Hall Lane and continue to the hall **(A)**.

Croxteth Hall

Just before reaching it, turn left along a tarmac track, at the start of the green-waymarked River Alt Trail. The track passes by a pool on the left and crosses a bridge at the end of another pool (Long Pond) on the right. At a green-waymarked post, turn left onto a path which turns right and continues through trees, keeping parallel to the track, and at the next post turn right to cross the track.

As you keep ahead along the right inside edge of woodland, there are fine views to the right across the open parkland. On reaching the River Alt **(B)** – little more than a brook here – turn right alongside it. The path forks but the two branches rejoin about 100 metres further on and you continue to a T-junction. Turn left to cross a bridge over the river, turn right to walk alongside its opposite bank and follow the main path as it curves left to reach a tarmac track.

Continue along the track, which bends right by an iron fence on the left and, at a small triangular green, turn left – here leaving the River Alt Trail – to join another track. Walk along this straight track, passing a Riding Centre on the right, which continues between Mull Wood (a nature reserve) on the left and, after passing beside a metal

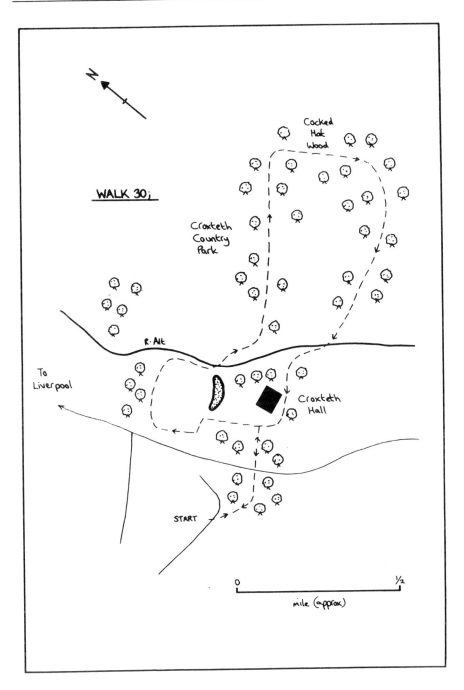

WALK 30;

Cocked Hat Wood

Croxteth Country Park

R. Alt

To Liverpool

Croxteth Hall

START

0   ½

mile (approx)

gate, Cocked Hat Wood on the right. On approaching houses, the track turns right to continue along the edge of the park through Cocked Hat Wood. Later it curves right again and on emerging from the trees, keep ahead – passing beside another metal gate – to a T-junction.

Turn right, cross the River Alt again – from here there is a fine view of Croxteth Hall ahead – and at a crossroads of tracks, keep ahead through a gate into the grounds of the hall **(C)**. The track curves left to another crossroads. Keep ahead and turn right beside the south wing of the hall to a T-junction.

Turn left, to rejoin the outward route and retrace your steps to the car park.

Features of Interest

(A) The architectural history of Croxteth Hall is quite complex. Originally an Elizabethan building, it has been extended and partially rebuilt several times as a reflection of the rising status and fortunes of its owners. The elegant facade of the south wing was built in the early 18th century and the west wing, where the present main entrance is, was completed between 1902 and 1904.

The hall was the home of the Molyneux family, later the Earls of Sefton, who were neighbours – and at one time rivals – of the Stanleys, the Earls of Derby, who lived literally just up the road at Knowsley. It was probably at its height in the Edwardian period just before the outbreak of the First World War. In 1952 some of the rooms were badly damaged by fire and twenty years later, following the death of the 7th and last earl, the hall passed into the ownership of Liverpool city council.

The tour of the hall, which includes the kitchens, servants' quarters and family rooms, really brings home to you, through imaginative reconstructions, what life was like here at the time of its Edwardian greatness, both as a servant and as a weekend house guest of Lord and Lady Sefton.

(B) The River Alt, just a narrow stream at this point, flows through the park, on through the northern suburbs of Liverpool and across the coastal plain to enter Liverpool Bay between Hightown and Crosby.

(C) In 1972 when the hall passed to Liverpool council, roughly half the grounds were sold for housing and the remaining half became the present country park. As well as the woodlands, pastures and formal gardens, there is a Victorian Walled Garden near the hall and the Home Farm; the latter has an important collection of rare farm breeds of the past.

Also of interest:

WALKS IN MYSTERIOUS LANCASHIRE

Delving into a host of mysterious places throughout Lancashire, Graham Dugdale's collection of 30 walks appeals to walkers with enquiring minds. Lucid walking directions and the author's ornate, hand-drawn maps complement the entertaining commentary. £6.95

TOWNS & VILLAGES OF BRITAIN: LANCASHIRE

Full of historical facts and liberally laced with tales of hauntings, witchery and enchantment - the moors, valleys and mossland of Lancashire are the backdrop to Michael Smout's comprehensive gazeteer of the county's towns and villages. "The histories of our towns and villages neatly gathered in one definitive guide" SOUTHPORT VISITER £8.95

BEST PUB WALKS IN LANCASHIRE

Lancashire has a rich pub heritage and a surprising variety of countryside for invigorating walks. This is the most comprehensive guidebook of its type. £6.95

BY-WAY BIKING IN LANCASHIRE

From Morecambe Bay to Bolton and from Blackpool to Burnley, Henry Tindell reveals Lancashire's outstanding potential as a destination for mountain bikers. 27 routes explore a fine variety of off-road tracks within easy reach of the large northern towns and cities. Henry has included some safe riding and easy trails suitable for the young and old. £6.95

LANCASHIRE MAGIC & MYSTERY

Covering all of Lancashire, including Merseyside and Greater Manchester, Ken Field's book guides you to places of mystery and curiosity. With tales of hauntings, witchcraft, religious relics, folklore and UFOs, this is a must for anyone interested in the supernatural. £6.95

WEST LANCASHIRE WALKS
No need to venture into touristy areas, it's all on the doorstep for Lancashire's walkers - "Knowledgeable guide to 25 rambles by the Ramblers' West Lancs Group Chairman" RAMBLING TODAY. £6.95

EAST LANCASHIRE WALKS
This companion volume to "West Lancashire Walks" leads you to an abundance of walking and places of interest which lie just beyond your urban doorstep to the East - a haunted house near Warrington, an American Wood at Aspel, there's even a giant on the banks of the Mersey! £6.95

BEST TEA SHOP WALKS IN LANCASHIRE
Breathtaking upland scenery, lush river valleys and impressive coastal paths - then complete your day by indulging in the celebrated English pastime of afternoon tea. £6.95

50 CLASSIC WALKS IN LANCASHIRE
Terry Marsh again shares his vast experience to explore the good walking country and places of beauty within the county's boundaries - known to the locals but waiting to be discovered by the wider population. £7.95

CHILLING TALES OF OLD LANCASHIRE
Set in Victorian Lancashire, here is a spine-chilling collection of tales - "...sure to thrill, chill and amaze" THE LANCASTER GUARDIAN. £6.95

JOURNEY THROUGH LANCASHIRE
This provides a close-up view of the people and places of Lancashire - "Packed with whimsy & wonder" THIS ENGLAND. £7.95

In case of difficulty, or for a free catalogue, please contact:
SIGMA LEISURE, 1 SOUTH OAK LANE, WILMSLOW, CHESHIRE SK9 6AR.
Phone: 01625-531035; Fax: 01625-536800.
E-mail: sigma.press@zetnet.co.uk .
Web site: http//www.sigmapress.co.uk
VISA and MASTERCARD orders welcome.